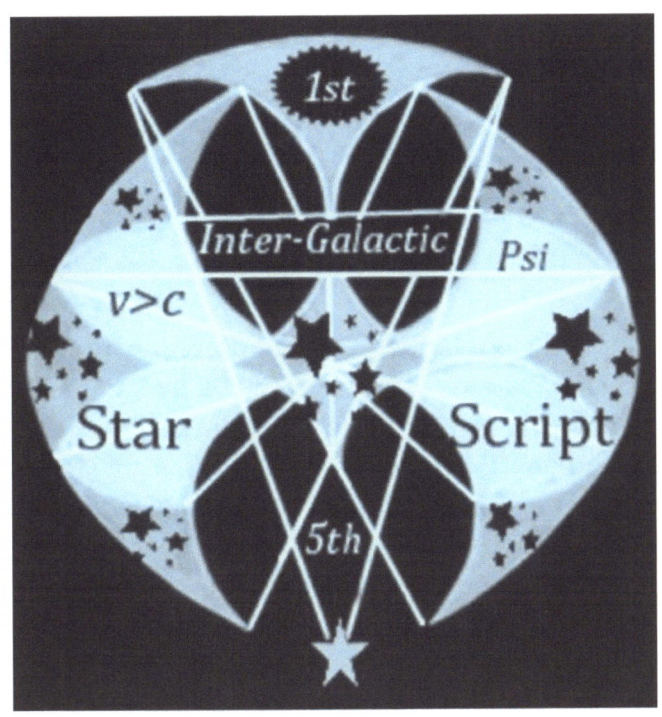

www.nuts4mars.com

Copyright (c) First Viewer 5th D 2009

ISBN# 9780981147079

Hyper-shift down to up, sighting on dots

Remarkably enough, I was admitted without prerequisites into the Math program at the University of Alberta based on my original creative manuscript, by the Chairman of the Math Department J. W. Macki, in 1986. For the first three months it all looked like chicken-scritching, then it finally resolved and I was able to enjoy the beauty and mystery of mathematics. I remained at the U. of A. for a few years studying a smattering of courses in math, physics, astronomy (still a favourite), and philosophy. I proceed, having faithfully retain my original manuscript and an ongoing interest in hyperspace. Alas, in practical terms, my math is now as cold as deep space or what I prefer to call, in the spirit of adventure, DeepSide. But, as if oblivious to this fact, the hyperspace paintings and visual geometry continue to spontaneously form. As a result I have written the following highly unusual account based on the original manuscript and including my recent works, specifically on hyperspace. This is the very strange account of an experience that began back in 1983. I was in my mid-twenties, living in the small but artistically encouraging city of Barrie. About an hours drive north of the more widely known city of Toronto, Ontario. Working by day at a Stained Glass shop. Cutting glass with my bare hands. A young passionate painter by night. Life was as sparkling and as full as the moon reflecting off the waters of a lake. Seen from my tiny room-with-a-view; both home and studio. One mid-summer night in July as I sat contentedly painting a truly extraordinary event happened. I was jolted out of my busy and rewarding artist's musing, when completely unexpected and for no apparent reason, I experienced two holographic images, in my mind. Distinct as cohesive units, or sure, wave packets of timelight info. The holograms were produced (received?) followed by very intense mental imagery. Urgently, I kept a written record of these holograms and the accompanying rapid onslaught of imagery. I followed intuitively where the images led my thought processes. I used a method of spontaneously recording the flow of mental images occurring quite insistently on the heels of the holograms. After the images I 'saw' were copied down, I developed a system to provide structure. Letting intuition be my guide. It wasn't until months later I came to recognize the first hologram was in fact a hypercube, the hyper sphere as the most likely fit.

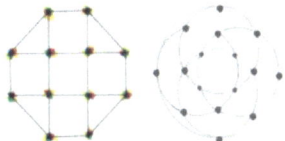

Shown here in 2 dimensional representations, they were at least four dimensional and resolved ultimately to contain a glimpse into a set that contains the 5th Dimension. Timelight plays an essential part in our 4D take on reality. (2009 Note: it was 5th D and SpaceTimeLight, connected and bent enabling Hypershift. Discernable using quantum psi exactly like Viewing as trained by the Military. See www.nuts4mars and 'Remote Viewing: Knights of Mars' as well as 'Remote Viewing: Ancient Links & Future Trails' for more in depth discussion and actual Remote Views in full color.) Shortly after experiencing the holograms, I became aware I was developing a good case of 'precognition' ability. The images themselves tended to display a natural focus an intent set on the future. It was an internally generated spontaneous revelation. Divine inspiration, like most art and science and discovery. Tapping into the other psi chi Remote Viewers echoing through the time distinct, Past, Present and Future. A nexus moment, involving multiple dimensional clarity. A 5th wave packet enhancement discovered by a correct and precise moment of focus.

Their most obvious difference was the holograms were remarkably brighter, as if a pure light had suddenly, and yet existing through a time interval of some duration, burst into being. Distinctly as if they were beamed in. Light on top of our own inner light. Or, is it beneath, at the core? The energy and its associated imagery provide possible grounds for directly connecting elements of the present to future. Elements, as certain perceptions could best be described as precognitive reveal otherwise hidden facets of the future. One possible explanation for these precognitive flashes of intuition is that the future is released by unfolding events and the future exists thereby, at least potentially, by means of the present. As the present depends on the past, so the future depends on the present. Certainly suggesting some energy overlap. Upon release of this energy there is injected into a conscious state of mind, knowledge logically recognized as arrived at by an intuitive process. During a somewhat fleeting moment of time the future pervades the present. If a person is perceptive or receptive to this, he or she would be aware of the future in the present. However, this experienced precognition is unlike the holographic images which can last in their entirety, capable of rigidity and/or fluidity of motion, for a noticeably longer period of time. In other words, the holograms have more substance. You can actually 'see' them in your mind, different from just knowing, or remembering, or conceiving. In this respect a precognitive dream which provides pictures and action could also be said to have more substance than knowing.

Though still not as intense as a hologram.

The accuracy of any foreknowledge arrived at by intuition is attested to by virtue of the events being actually encountered at a later time, as determined by our usual notion of linear time. Thus the images are comparable to the effective confluence or the change of direction of perception which is characteristic of hyper-structures. As for example, 4D hypercubes and hyperspheres which permit us to shift our visual range. They provide a means for a spontaneous reversal of order, whereby our perception of the front becomes the back. With hyperstructure the spontaneous change of direction can be achieved from any point. In terms of 3D space, a reversal of direction along the line of sight is inherent in the structure, say of the sphere. Provided there is an 'extension' or 'gap' between the points of sight. Here the effect of a gap or an extended distance between positions of the points of view becomes apparent. Clearly, hyper-structures demonstrate the characteristic of reversal. Since 3D is a subspace of 4D and hence could contain similar components, this allows for the characteristic of reversal, as incorporated into both 3D and 4D as well.

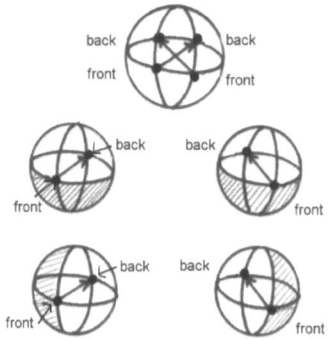

The ability to form holographic images in the mind is one of nature's givens. No gizmos or attachments necessary. When images occur we may resolve how we intuitively perceive and rationally accept our nature of dimensions. The subsequent unfolding of patterns is perhaps in response to the stimulus provided by the holograms, as basic recognition of the inter-dimensional extent of these images comes into play. As with hyperspace, holograms display the existence of extra dimensions to our senses. For the very essence of their structure (any part of a hologram reflects the whole) allows us a brief glimpse of all sides of the coin from one position. By virtue of their being experienced internally and interpreted selectively by individuals, mental images are presumably individualistic. Perhaps we share as a species a common or innately recognizable system of organized structural pattern resulting from a base underlying our thought process. A viable link between us and the dimensionality of space/time, could be established by such a base. Is this base determined by dimensions?

A cube's three dimensions would be noted algebraically as having a standard basis. Our mind's inner realm could also be composed of a standard basis. Our awareness of the 4th dimension rules out a mental structure based solely on the 3rd dimension. The 4th dimension includes our familiar 3rd as a subspace. The 4th dimension could provide a suitable dimensionality for us to experience space/time. However, as 3D is linked to 4D, then 4D may be linked to 5D, and so on. In theory the mental range would appear to be possibly limitless since we can conceive of the notion of infinity. But the standard basis of the experienced mental structure might be defined in terms of its being limited, or as covering a set range, where dim R n, $0 < n < $ infinity. Although we readily acknowledge man's perception of four dimensions as we are all aware of time and space, more dimensions could be incorporated in our mind's basic structure albeit our contact with such could be at subliminal or superliminal levels. If it is what we have knowledge of, that forms the prerequisite for a basis to our mental structure then there would be no fixed common basis other than that which is agreed upon or commonly accepted. Also, a base reflecting merely our belief system would limit the number of dimensions to 4, as realized and observed. Our knowledge of a certain dimensionality of this base or foundation, could impose such as a limit. Thus forming structure and presenting order to us. But, if our familiar base as also linked *holographically* to other higher dimensions, this might allow for random fluctuations in our experience. And with more dimensions at play you could then consider whether two elements could be aware of the same event at the same time. As exhibited by synchronicity where two events, seemingly separate, could actually be connected. Each event, although they seem separate in terms of 4D, may be linked with a direct correspondence in a higher dimension. It could be because of such an essential inter-dimensional aspect to the base that our minds are able to hold a fix on our shifting view of reality. Our multidimensional base playing a functional role of some significance. As it is by its connection we may experience these glimpses involving higher dimensions of reality. An individual's perception of reality would be distinct from another person's perception of events, but with a shared cohesive inter-dimensional structure which forms the essence of our existence. With a base set on 4D and linked to higher dimensions, mental images would provide us with the means to understand and apply the variance of spatial and temporal components of reality, nature. If there is a common basis to our minds, then this would explain how we are all different yet can communicate and understand one another. One of the most significant attributes we share as beings is our perception of time (including timelessness). How can the mind perceive something so all pervading yet so elusive as time? Perhaps it is because time forms part of this common basis inherent in the structure of the mind. Physically we are only aware of living in a 3D space since we don't physically feel time- we feel only time's effects.

The process of growth and decay provide a biological means of determining the effects of time thereby including 4D in our circumstances. Certain physical aspects show our contact with the 4th dimension by the effects of time, but it is through some internal means that we understand and deal with the ramifications of time. An internal sense of time and the external effects of time are both comprehensible to us by applying our mind's innate, as well as learned, knowledge. We certainly do possess information involving more than our observable 3D. Mental images take time to form and provide a suitable link between what the mind knows of itself and what the mind relates to itself. It follows that in order for us to mentally gain access to more than 3D we would need an intermediary as offered by mental imagery. Time is an essential part of a life and unless you can survive without realizing some means of relating to time, then mental images are perhaps necessary for survival itself. Regarding the concept of a common base, according to Dr. Rudy Rucker ('The 4th Dimension' p.145) "... At any moment the world 'gives' us a collection of sights, sounds, smell, and so on. By a more or less unconscious process, we organize these sensations into a stable framework. This background framework, which everyone agrees on, is reality: a continuum of 3 space dimensions and 1 time dimension." Which does not exclude the possibility that there is a whole that our framework or structure is but a part of. So, we could each have our own individual brain-holograms which are linked to a grand Hologram. Immanuel Kant (1724-1804 philosopher) was one of the first philosophers concerned with higher dimension. He saw space/time as the pre-form of all sensible intuition.

Since hyperspace is intrinsically linked to space/time, a hyperspace holographic model of space/time could be considered a reflection of this pre-form. Makes a good case for the necessity, or at least benefit, using intuition directly when exploring hyperspace.

Intuitive-Logic

In addition to the occurrence of original symbols, there is a system which we use to interpret or read, in order to gain insight, understanding, comprehension, perception..., this being the 'language of thought'. Arising from intuitive logic. And, intuitive logic entails symbols- evidence of this intimate link to creation. Each of us being created and in turn being able to create. If intuitive logic is 'how' we read the images, the process could be considered a highly abstracted level of analysis. The philosopher Aristotle (384-322 BC) wrote, it is by light that we distinguish colors. Then Aristotle's view is that recognition arises from the knowers repeated experience through contact with the external world. However, I think that we recognize another experience as well, that of an internal nature which directly concerns our intellectual insights. As Immanuel Kant, the great German philosopher, states-'The understanding cannot intuit anything, and the senses cannot think anything. Only through their union can knowledge arise. Hence the term 'intuitive-logic'." Which makes sense, since the human brain is divided into two halves - the left side perceives the world in a linear manner and the right side perceives whole patterns; the left functions logically and the right function intuitively. I was using both left and right sides of the brain to 'see' the lines of the hologram. With an underlying structure from which the images are formed, the mind recognizes patterns/events in between the images, and then proceeds to use intuitive logic to reveal the underlying abstract principles. Then the abstract principles are assimilated into our thoughts and experience, by virtue of these images induced in our mind. The images themselves being generated abstract principles. Which would explain the pattern 'recognition'. Our grasp of the abstract principles originating from our overall shared experience with multi-dimensions. Common related experience derived from common abstract principles embodied in this underlying structure, which in turn leads to common images. In effect, directly experiencing the images leads to the retrieval of those basic abstract principles, or archetypes, possessed by humans. The basic structure then provides connections for the mind to elaborate on, creating even more abstract principles. As shown by the ability of our species to imagine and to grow. In this respect, using intuitive logic is rather like when you get an idea and write it down, and when you read what you've written this leads to more ideas. Only, in this case the mind is using images as its 'mark' (or ordering process). We 'read' in the language of intuitive logic about our common reality. As images bridge the gap between what is essentially there, and what it is that we know about what is there. Intuition tapping into the otherwise hidden regions of our mind's perceptions and logic following from our ability to reason and make connections. It seems combined intuition and logic gives us knowledge about what is revealed from the past balanced with what is realized about the future.

<u>Precognition</u>

It is when we grasp a specific from our general knowledge derived from the structure, which links to a corresponding specific in actions or events which later experience, that the element of precognition comes into play.

Precognition could be described as the process whereby a specific realized in a present time frame of 'now', in the mind, links directly with a specific event or action, in a later or future time frame, that takes place outside the mind. Precognition is evident when you are aware of knowledge of the occurrence before it happens. This overall process is in accordance with our use of intuitive logic and its influence. Certain pertinent images suffuse the mind as precognitive flashes of insight, given merit using intuitive logic.

    Our chosen awareness of an event is either based on what we know by previous experience, leading to current experience, as determined by cause and effect, or it is based on acknowledging the characteristic prescience of the senses associated with the future. Concerning the importance of the role of mental imagery in regards to precognition, consider the following - human beings are by nature mobile creatures.

You could think of the body as being a vehicle which permits the individual (the passenger) to move through its surrounding space/time. Even when stationary the life processes constitute movement. Inside this vehicle, the mind could be considered a receptacle of knowledge. Within this receptacle images are produced which in turn enable us to traverse freely among abstract principles or events that relate to our experiences of the past, present and future. Images permit the motion of the abstract principles within the mind. Just as the body ceases to move without a mind, the abstract principles would cease to have relevance by means of motion or thoughts within the mind if there were no images. Since the abstract principles provide knowledge in regards to specifics relating to the individual's reality in space/time, and the abstract principles are dependent on images for our understanding. It follows, mental images are *essential* in order for human individuals to mentally experience a viable link to space/time. Furthermore, the philosopher John Locke, in 'An Essay Concerning Human Understanding' presents the idea that extension is inherent rather than merely observed. According to Locke, ('Place, Extension, and Duration') we "...can have no idea as to the place of the universe, though we can of all the parts of it...but all beyond it is one uniform space or expansion." Distance is here defined as being between 2 points, and expansion as between 3 points. Using the mathematical term of 'absolute' distance (where the distance is measured as the same in both directions within an absolute frame), then the distance between two points becomes mirrored as an extension within itself. Indeed, this is displayed by hyperspace as visually observable reversals of direction. Whereas John Locke regards thinking and extension as separate, I believe thinking could be considered a form that extends itself, albeit internally, by creation. But, Locke also says, " Extension includes no solidity nor resistance to the motion of body, as body does." Well, thinking is not solid, so it seems his view of 'extension having no solidity' would lean more towards thinking as including extension rather than being separate from extension.

<u>Reversed Time</u>

A future point is introduced into the present via movement along a time frame. This movement enables visions of the future (ie: an intense moment of the future's present) to be displaced or interjected into another dimensional time slot. That is, to take a point of intensity from within the future, and travel with it in any direction. Willing it to the past or the future with equal intensity. Clarity is of main importance here. If you can focus and get a vision, you can direct it into the past or the future. Since perhaps it is not just the present that has a past and a future attached- the future has a past/present/future as well. Essentially a future moment becomes a present moment. As happens when looking at a Necker cube.

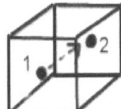 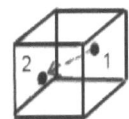   Necker cubes

When seeing dot 1 as being at the front and dot 2 as at the back of the cube, we see 1 as the present and 2 as the future since it is farther back or later, along. the line of sight. Now, seeing dot 2 as the front of the cube it becomes the present and dot 1 is the future. When our mind does the mental flip of perception, time can be fleetingly sensed as running forwards/backwards, as the front becomes the back and the back becomes the front. So, in this example in order to determine or sense the content or events relevant to the next/future, moments, you would only need to be able to cross the gap between the past and the future. Quantum physics currently exhibits this principle as it includes time- reversible equations.   Next, is a diagram referring to an inter-linear/dimensional (inclusive) motion between inter co-ordinated elements of an alternate real time, through spatial relation.

<u>Mirror Imaging</u>

Another distinctive feature that arose from my applying intuitive logic after 'seeing' the holograms, was the use of mirror imaging. As Dr. R. Rucker states ('The Fourth Dimension Houghton Mifflin, 1985), "What makes the Necker cube reversal so important is that the 2 possible 3D interpretations of the original skeleton drawing are in fact mirror images of each other."

Additionally, concerning hyperspherical space, Dr. Rucker explains the mirror reversal process as "... assume that the Sphereland light rays move around the spherical space in great circles .... all the light rays that start out from Square's body re-cross each other at the opposite side of the sphere. This means that Square will see a bunch of images of pieces of his body over on the other side of the sphere, and as it turns out, these images will fit together to make a ghost image of himself, upside down and mirror reversed." (image from 'Geometry, Relativity and the 4th D' by R. Rucker)

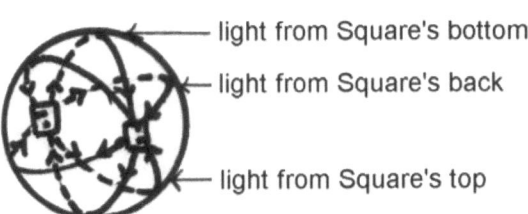

Focused Direction and Concentration Patterns

It is true that ordinarily you have to think about the past (using recall, memory, etc.) in other words consciously direct your thoughts backwards to retrieve information. Granting as well that sometimes events of the past just come into your consciousness unbidden, or spontaneously. By the same token, perhaps knowledge of events from the future can spontaneously form in the mind and we can, by directing a conscious choice of acknowledgment, be then aware of these 'future' thoughts. Countless thoughts, pictures and images pass by our mind's eye. It is up to the individual to determine which thoughts we grasponto and attach any significance to. Dr. Rudy Rucker touches on this focusing of the direction of our attention when he said a good place to start ones efforts to develop a 4D consciousness is using mental exercises that lead to a sensation of timelessness. The system of intuitive logic presented here appears to evoke a similar concentration pattern. Helping to slip into a state of timelessness. A timeless state may be just another way of saying atemporal or beyond linear time. (Note: timelight appears to be multi-dimensional with the hyper shift breaking the barrier of timelight speed).

Perhaps precognition is not so much a display of latent psychic ability as an option we all share, once you permit the influence and don't reinforce the bland shield of denial about our ability to know truths from the future.

Perspective: Point of view

Consider a point of view above or outside of the defined area's position, elements as not seen as only on one plane. A point outside of form represents a perspective of seeing things from a point in the space outside the form itself, which is what one does when looking at something. Whether physical objects or words on a page, one sees an area of defined space, form, which is in turn surrounded by a space. Also, seeing both of these by the act of looking as it were, through Space. The area in-between defining a limit. This perspective is used when the viewer and object are considered to be on the same plane. There is a line of sight from form to form. Distance or measurement of the line becomes relevant. The distance between object and eye and again from the eye to the area in the brain where an image of the object is formed. This also implies a concept of distance in the brain. Rather than seeing objects as being separate and apart in the universe, it is actually a chosen common belief that things are so limited. In the cosmic scheme of things, perhaps all is connected.

The physical object is apart from the physical eye, yet an image is received in the brain as the object. This area between the object and the eye is a space, or physical gap - implying distance. To cross this distance is to higher, one looking down would see both the forms and the space in-between. Without having to travel from form to form through a direct line of sight. It would then be from plane to plane. There is an existing agreed upon chosen system of belief, as seeing things as being separate or apart in our physical universe. However, seeing things as having no limits except those imposed by a belief system removes the limit. This does not describe a condition of utter chaos, as it is a being, a person, deciding to believe that there are no limits other than those imposed by will to create form. To remove the limits by believing things to have no limits (implied chaos), realize that at the same time the very act of believing itself imposes the limits. Since the act of belief is limited to the individual's belief system. This due to everyone having a unique perception and interpretation of reality. In other words, limits are set by deciding where to place them when defining a belief system. To contain an area of thought within an area of reference, for thoughts to take shape, the concepts must be in clear packages. It is possible then to select a package and form a unit of thought from the elements contained in the package or concept. Belief is composed of which elements in the package are selected and focused on. Concepts may hold our beliefs, whereby our thoughts are limited, but beliefs are only limited by which concept is accessed. A link or connection is apparent between our thoughts and structured concepts. To some degree, our *beliefs* set our limits. Providing us a means to hold or shift how we understand and respond to our perceived reality structure. Because belief, itself, is flexible within our conceptual range. Our individual conditions and information contribute to our beliefs, and these of course change. And our concepts are thus linked, as well. Perhaps connected, too, to an overriding structure, which is in turn connected to a great overall common consciousness shared version of Reality. Thus, our thoughts are part of the whole, and may define for a time the basics of the whole, but they are allowed to include progress and creation and new knowledge.

Our paradigms can and do shift. Human's view of the state of the world itself went from being 2 dimensional, flat, to a round spherical shaped planet. A bit like 20/20 hindsight, once society does these major shifts.

Considering the ultimate basic structure to be holographic is regarded by Immanuel Kant ('Critique of Reason') as differing from the norm. Kant reasoned, "It is the nature of our intelligence to proceed in knowledge from an analytical universal, or a conception, to the particular as given in empirical perception. The multiplicity of the latter thus remains undetermined, until judgment has determined it by bringing the perception under the conception. We may, however, conceive of an intelligence different in kind from ours, an intelligence which is perceptive and not discursive and which therefore proceeds from a synthetic universal to the particular, that is, from a perceived whole to the parts. For such an intelligence, the connection of the parts which form a determinate whole would not be, or appear, contingent as it is for us ... But from a peculiar character of our intelligence, a real whole in nature is regarded only as the effect of the combined motive forces of the parts.". Kant continues…"We may, however, instead of viewing the whole as dependent of the parts, after the manner of our discursive intelligence, take a perceptive or archetypal intelligence as our standard, and seek to comprehend the dependence of the parts on the whole, both in their specific nature and in their interconnection.

I feel this reinforces the notion that it is because the images are but parts of the whole, the source, that when I received them they were less intense, but still extreme in themselves, than the startlingly clear and bright holograms themselves.

In this work, I have tried to do a sort-of reverse -engineering, starting with the holograms, and then the images and trying to sort out the connections and meanings I was able to determine. One result of my effort was the original visual work on hyperspace, found in section three in this book. Curiously enough, it appears to relate to spaceflight. Appropriate enough, if indeed Aliens from space were involved. (note: it was not until 2006 I was involved in Stargate Viewing.)

Particularly the macrocosmic space/time shortcut, as presented by Mr. F. Loup and others in his ilk cutting edge speculative physics. The links to his work (currently only a mock-up at CERN, although he has been previously published by the scientific community) may be found, ready to click, on the Hyperspace Gallery page of my site at www.nuts4mars.com

Really a fascinating read, even if you skip through the math and go for the gist of it. Of course, the same could be said for this piece of RV work. You may find it interesting even, or especially, if you skip reading the first section containing an attempted explanation, and just go straight for the meat- the Images found in the next section. **2008**: no Alien and/or manifestation as of yet. Just kidding. However, there are clear signs of a Star Trail *system* that follows along and decodes specifically as this manner of visually rendering using sensed or psi precognition. As such, it develops along using intuitive-logic, to find the connection points and linking for lines. Providing a means to decode the messages and descriptive visuals, since this is the usual precognitive Remote Viewing Theme application. The RV process is always linking to and revealing in Time Context relevant means.

Like any typical Remote Viewing or RV. The same system is used and shows connections in specific ancient Egyptian RV visuals. Here in their ancient recordings, the visual Time Vision language of their hieroglyphs, we are given the means to decode hyper shift information. Reading like a quasi- manual, and considering the direct referencing to digital and computer knowledge as well as the visuals of the nuclear cooling towers, and other present links that we can relate to, it is definitely RV. Perhaps, even more astounding, it is also linked to interstellar messaging. Signs of outer Solar influence and direction. I find I can follow along with their tale and descriptive content, using the system as it was understood and developed in the following pages. It took months of extreme receptivity and intensely focused energy and attention, will even, if you like to record. Then it took many years to pull it together into the fashion it made it into here. Crude, difficult, not an easy task. If it looks rough around the edges, it was a lot of rougher. Think of it as a wild raw continuous stream of imagery with outstanding or decidedly noticeable, points of retention. And not only receiving the imagery itself, but also attempting to follow along and discern how and when and what, about the imagery receiving method, itself. I was unlayering superimposed and combined and inter-dimensionally sorting as well as merely recording spontaneous mental imagery. It was an intricate and immersive endeavour requiring precision guidance and great faith in the creative, with always, the good LORD as the ultimate overseer. Way before I read and then re-read and understood with the lifting of the veil, the instructions to 'See' presented in the Holy Bible, under Jeremiah One. Later expanded on under Jeremiah 50.

This work led to my RV of Mars accomplishment, and my eventual understanding of the RV phenomenon. Then, to my greater surprise, it is also used as a system to decode the messages of that ancient and precise piece of RV the 'Chariot' papyrus, specifically. See 'Remote Viewing: Ancient Links & Future Trails' also at my RV site, URL above. Fascinating in itself, and potentially inter-stellar as well as inter-dimensional. Maybe time portals, not just teleports are in our future. God's Universe doesn't disappoint the faithful.

The experts have conferences about Extra Dimensions. Exchanged ideas world wide, in 2004 and 2005 and nothing up for recent. They did not all stop being interested. I say Teleports are already here. Conspicuously quiet. They're on the verge. All kinds of recent years breakthroughs, too. They have twisted lasers and all kinds of goodies they didn't back in '05...anytime now, I figure...some new form of instantaneous or damn close to it, travel...oil might become a dinosaur sooner not later.
Other previous work done by G. Kalbermann (1) and H. Halevi (2), (1) Faculty of Agriculture and Racah Institute of Physics, Hebrew University, Jerusalem, Israel, Cyclotron Institute, Texas (2) Jerusalem, Israel. "Concerning: 'Nearness Through An Extra Dimension- It is shown that if our visible universe is a thin trapped shell in a five-dimensional universe, all matter in it may be connected almost instantaneously through the fifth dimension. 'What appears to be action at a distance is then understood as undetectable ultra fast communication. '...'the trapped universe is essentially flat',(According to the fairly recent findings of the WMAP project, it was determined the shape of the Universe is indeed flat. The scientists needed to know the shape in order for greater accuracy in their many calculations and theories. I think it was mostly for their cosmological constant, a figure they use for things like red-shift and blue-shift. Here too.)...'Our universe then becomes a thin shell in a larger hyper-universe'...'regardless of the mechanism of trapping, its very existence implies that all matter in the universe may be connected through the fifth dimension by means of electromagnetic (or other) signals in an undetectable amount of time. All matter and energy in the universe is then tied up together in a manner that usual locality and

causality on the shell would prohibit. This may in turn explain not only phenomena related to quantum mechanical behaviour, but also macroscopic action at a distance. One can picture this view by thinking of the matter in the universe as puppets connected by cables to a puppeteer that holds all the strings together. A perturbation in one of the strings causes a turmoil in almost zero time to all the other strings. In the next section a simple model proves these assertions…', 'action at a distance is, in our opinion, a mirage, the real situation is an incessant bombardment by ultra fast radiation that fills the universe shell."

The term -ultra fast- being of some importance here. I do think of this in terms of superluminal motion. Things that move at c, the speed of light, or *faster*. What they are calling simply, ultra fast, likely in order to not exceed c. I will now call it Viewing at c, or Light Viewing. Oh, and don't get all excited by the words turmoil etc. they are not talking catastrophe, here. This is about light and particles. When they use terms like signature, you don't look for ink. Here is a form of science lingo and understood meaning applied. I look for basic concepts. Most of it is over my head of course with the actual math/physics. I am colder than cold and not in doing math. You are either doing it or you are not. There isn't much for in-between. You can however, look to the surrounding concepts, their theories are dealing with in these applied experiments.

'Collapse is prevented by the pressure of the mass in the shell, although space where the matter is sparse could be easily penetrated by the inner and outer regions producing important effects. One such effect could be similar to that provided by the hypothetical dark matter. Instead of having more matter inside the galaxies that is unseen, there could be unseen negative mass outside them. **Also, if the shell is cracked suddenly and mass from the inner and outer regions coalesces with the mass in the shell they could annihilate producing enormous bursts of energy** an alternative to black hole generated active galactic nuclei. Hence $F=G$(to the minus 1)$=1 + kx$(squared). K greater than 0. The constant of the harmonic potential is unknown. However, the potential should be enormously steep for the shell to be of microscopic size. It should be smaller than the radii of nuclei, smaller than the deep inelastic scattering scale of the experiments carried until now, otherwise, its signature should have become visible'…etc….'so if the signal climbs up the harmonic potential and back far enough in x, the coordinate time becomes negligible. For example, $x=10$ (to the fifteenth)m, and $L=100$Mpc(mega parsecs, a star distances measurement) the time taken by radiation to traverse this cosmic distance is **$t=10$(to the minus fourth) sec.** A ridiculous time as **compared to the 326 Million years** needed for the light to traverse this distance along the direction perpendicular to R on the surface. (on the surface, $x=0$)'

No comparison. Arriving at a fraction of a second, rather than 326 Million years otherwise. And this, I know is possible. I do it every day, when I sit down to paint.

And in conclusion, they state:'In summary, if our universe is a thin shell immersed in a higher dimensional hyper universe, and if the shell is trapped by some repulsive force or analogous mechanism, then what seems to be action at a distance, such as the action of static potentials could be due to action through the fifth dimension.'

This has nothing to do with things collapsing and dark matter as a dark force like Darth Vadar in Star Wars. I found the lines in my poem 'Dragon Trails' (see 'MYST') an RV Theme on this trail, -**'pressures released by cracks in the shell of the egg'**; further along in the same article. You have to read the work from Israel about hyperspace, to understand the RV theme links.

 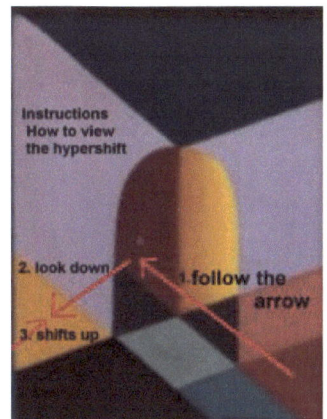 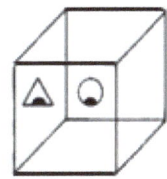

'Hyperspace Door' 2001; 1. Look up & in 2. Look down 3. Shifts up; standard Necker Cube

How to see a hyper-shift or visual Leap:
When looking at the painting, you should experience a spontaneous shift in visual perspective - one moment it is like looking into the door the next moment it seems to shift and appears like the left half of the painting is hanging suspended in space. The same as when you are looking at a Necker cube and the front reverses with the back. Here, on canvas, space/time is manipulated on a visual level. In effect, we experience a visual link to an extra dimension. Hyperspace travel might be one way to get around the obstacles of direct flight through space at speeds greater than light speed (due to impacts, and strange zones, and who knows what all is out there). To really go planet hopping in different star systems you need to ride those higher dimensions.
In Hyperspace, here becomes there with relative ease. For hyper physics by Fernando Loup see my work on hyperspace up on my site from pre -Stargate RV. We view a hyperspace shift by the use of sight, so perhaps the shift itself, being instantaneous implies a faster than light component. Before heading out to the wild black yonder you might want to practice planet hopping - using FTL perhaps - in our local solar system.

A central feature of the original oil painting 'Immersion' is, as well as the visual hyper shift in the background, there was an apparent time shift as well.

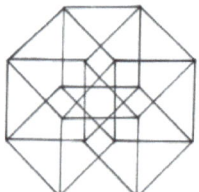 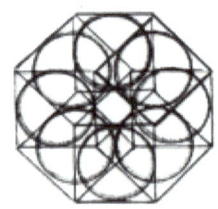 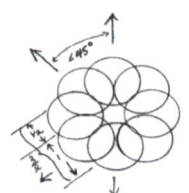 

Hypercube; Hypersphere (-from circles within Hypercube)

When another set of spheres (ie:circles) is added at a 45 degree angle to the 1st set, you get the shape in #1 which when rotated 45 degrees as in #2, becomes the same as an extended version #3.

Hyperspace Visual Extensions
Both extension and mirroring (a simultaneous reversal in direction) are properties exhibited visually by hyperspace. The Universe is expanding (as evidenced by the observed 'redshift' discovered by Hubble in the 1920's, also the Hubble telescope (1998), the universe is discovered by Hubble in the 1920's, also the Hubble telescope (1998), the universe is not only expanding but accelerating. Hyperspace also exhibits properties of expansion through visual extension.

MIRROR IMAGING A visual (perceptual) 4D shift or movement appears instantaneous. Appears to divide regions of hyperspace.

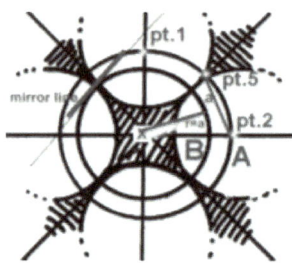

2D center of a Hypersphere:
Draw a circle A, divide into 8 equal sections, set compass to length of 'a' (ie: a=distance from pt.5 to pt.2) eg: center compass at pt.5 and draw a semi-circular sweep between pt. 1&2, do the same sweep all the way around, between pts. 1&2,2&3... Then draw a circle with compass on original center 'x', with radius=a.

They use 10 to the minus 35m, as the Planck radius. The other dude up on my Immersion/Hyperspace Gallery page, won the Max Planck award. And of course, Mr. Loup's work came after Kalbermann and Halvei, built on the -Macroscopic SpaceTime Shortcut in the Manyfold Universe- (2004). Work including within it, -'Enlarging the Bulk Dimension from the Planck Length to a Macroscopical size -the Dutch Equation.'-

A concept again, dealing initially with incredibly small. The Extra Dimensional 5th, a route. I think of it as extemporaneous. Outside of Time. And this paper in particular arrived at a throat or opening, with the size at R=square root of 2, times 10 and in my use of Minkowski to interpret the 4th into 2d, with my visual hyperspace diagrams, based on extension, I had it as R=square root 2. No times 10. I think he wanted to take a small army with him. Maybe he saw the Hole on Mars, eh?

As a word, sure, but so far as quantum mechanics…are you aware that all things, everything has spin, when it comes to the particles? Everything. So, of course not. If I was typing and used the word Ball and they had round ornaments, would that mean I was linked? No. Remote Viewing requires skill as well as psychic talent.

As to the issue of spin, as mentioned, the article was actually just explaining to you that they didn't have to like measure or know how each piece was spinning, what direction. In fact they found the wave packets were reintroduced identically, with unknown or unmeasured as for spin, etc. effects. It doesn't make any difference in other words. What goes in, as a spin in a certain direction comes out with the same spin. Etc. 1 (ok, maybe this does explain the repositioning not of the actual draw to the same rock, on Mars, but it might help explain why the actual View the next time, was facing in the same direction. Now, that would be possibly related to wave packets of reality-info keeping their same spin directions. To face in the same direction. I can tell it faced the same by the View matching the pointed in direction of the Rock, seen as a pointer. It pointed Right. For what was in front of that Rock, according to the actual photographs sent back via the Rover.

I imagine it all goes into the blend. Like spicing in soup. Total tea leaf reading with sensitive cohesion at that level. Only visible within the view range of a reader. Interpreted according to their knowledge and the Time Context relevant links. What it means depends on the issues it corresponds to with a direct link within an absolutely defined time frame. My freeze frames coming into play. Freeze motion, not freeze as in temperature. Like the stop motion and the layering that a video cam and software can do. There are often not only superimposed layers of visual content but also additional layers of descriptive elements. You can see color matches, pattern and shape matches. Also, you can make out tales that you can empathically relate to. It is a sense or feeling from reading and connecting to the story and emotion connecting to it. Composition and tension being as they are in the world of artistic creativity. Painting, writing, and movies in particular, light, form, color and sound combined provide excellent means of reproducing the wave packets of reality. A medium that responds readily to the necessary constraints and discipline of capturing the spirit and sensitivity for portraying these Quantum Chromo Dynamics.

Remote View paintings: 'Starfire' Oil 1983; 'Abstract Girl' Oil 1984

'Immersion' 27"x33" 2004; View match to top left in the photo looking out from a Military aircraft

'10,000 BC' movie excerpt match to View close up of flint arrow in foreground of Immersion

painting above left.

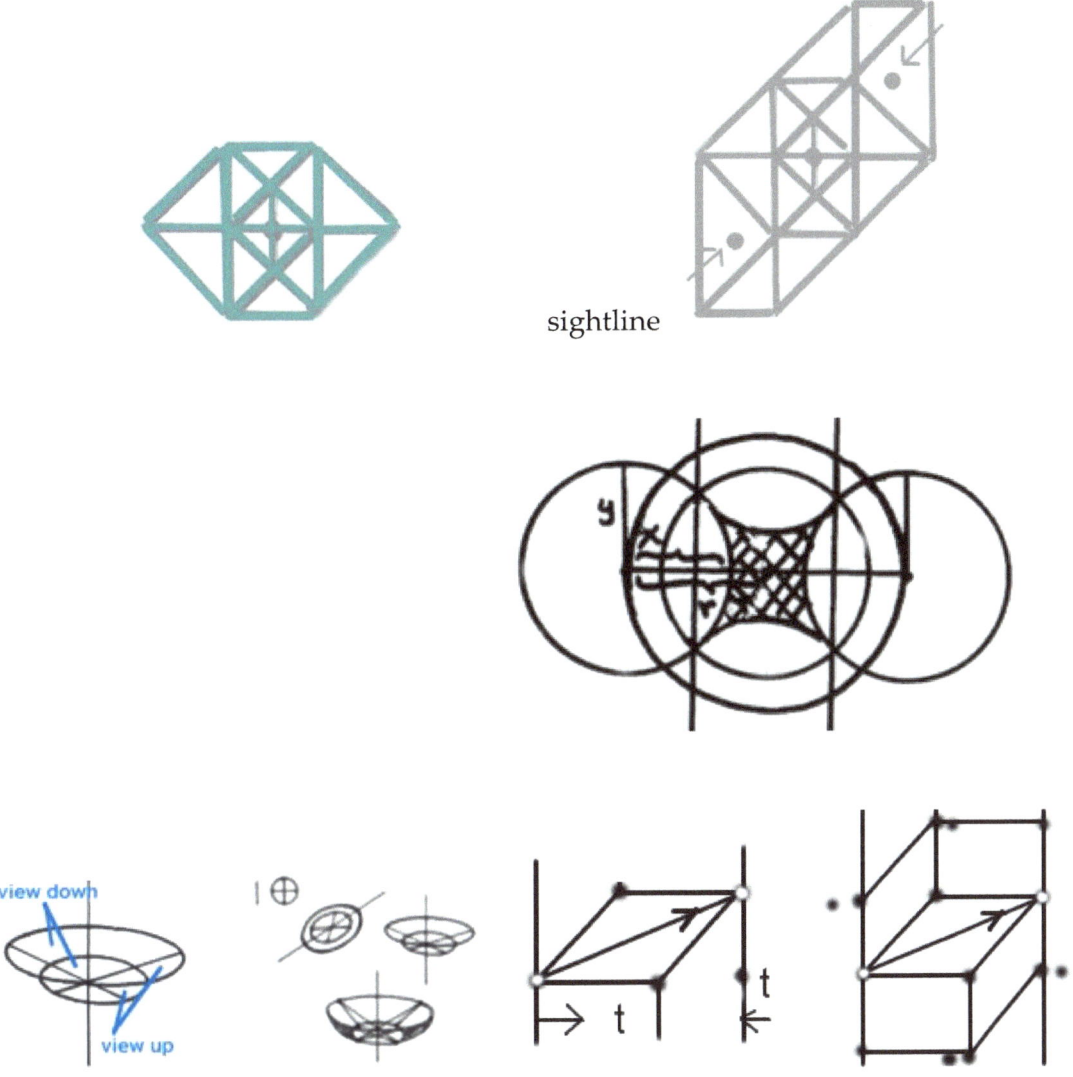

sightline

Selection of 'shift diagrams' enabling hyper shift visual leap; (center) hyper shift diagrams showing a 'freeze frame' to view a leap, using Minkowski's fundamental axiom - 'the substance at any world point may always with the appropriate determination of space & time be looked upon as at rest'. With Minkowski's 'at rest' there is no Lorentz treatment needed for equations. Similarly to 'view' a leap motion, like the inner workings of a Necker shift, there is a natural shift point where $v=t=0$ of course, a 'freeze frame', so we can connect to information containing links to SpaceTimeLight moments of 'other' times or what I call Elsewhere/when.

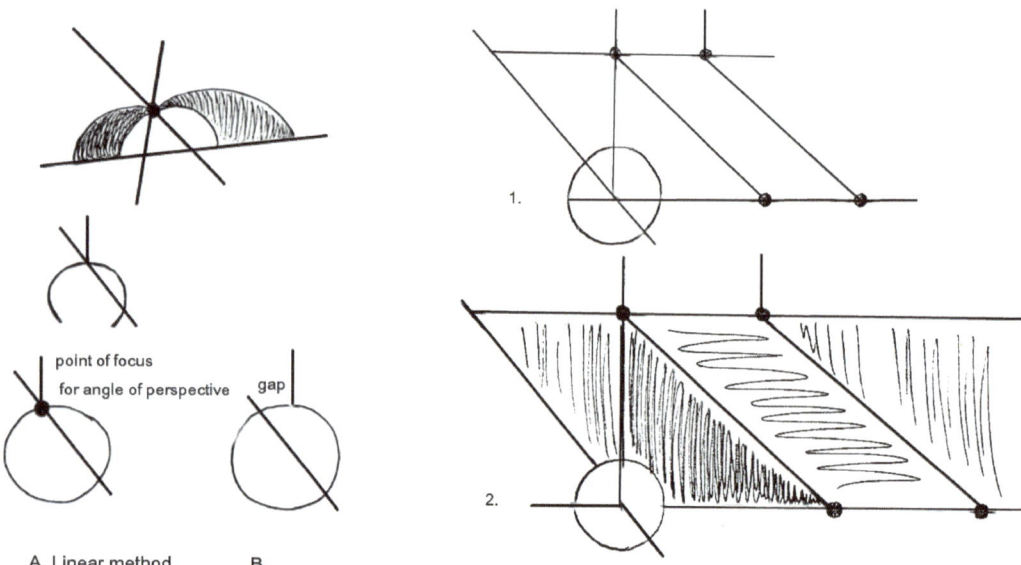

point of focus for angle of perspective   gap

A. Linear method   B.

1. To 'gap' is to make more connections available. To add another dimension wtih the increased perspective. With distance/space, there is a different angle of perspective, possible angles. Opens another area of information to the senses.

2. direction of focusing top right
   lines of thought
   connections/ bridge, shape

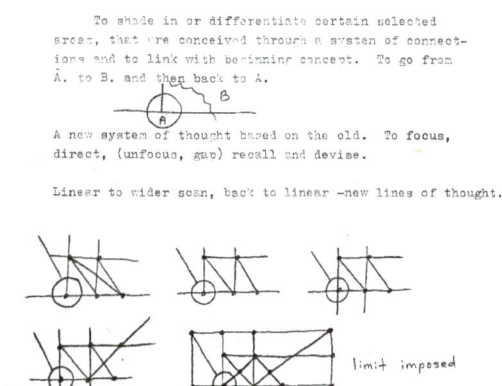

To shade in or differentiate certain selected areas, that are conceived through a system of connections and to link with beginning concept. To go from A. to B. and then back to A.

A new system of thought based on the old. To focus, direct, (unfocus, gap) recall and devise.

Linear to wider scan, back to linear —new lines of thought.

axis of agreement   limit imposed
greater area of reference - from image to system   extension of majorlines of thought.

Greater area of references- from image to events.

(at right) excerpt 'Remote Viewing: Ancient Links & Future Trails' by 1st 5th & Ingo Swann.

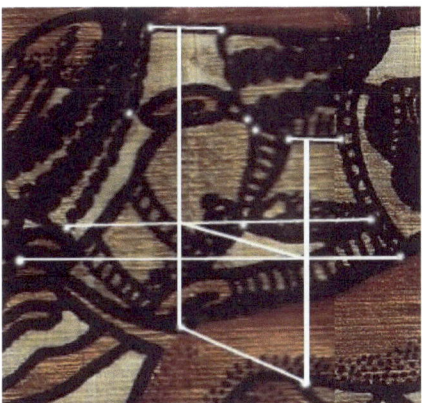

Excerpt from 'Chariot' papyrus; the dot system is as described in 'RV: Ancient Links & Future Trail's, and determined to psi matched precision according to time context. A Quantum Leap, very typical of RV for it's *descriptive* ability using 5th Dimensional properties.

Chariot papyrus View excerpt; tangent point on orb aim descriptive for 5th D visuals

MARS RACE between NASA's Phoenix Mar's Surface Lander and the Psi-chi View talent of 1st 5th: excerpted concept from the previously written account in 'Remote Viewing: Knights of Mars' at www.nuts4mars.com -I did not sit to paint then, it was near done when I sat to paint …that's why I always say I almost missed it! I was mucking around doing something else. I did not ever say nor is it true, that it was 'at orbit' like a race line when I started. Tell them to lay off the crack they are smoking. Stop bleeping with the truth. There were many witnesses I was not alone here when it happened and we all know I barely made it finished and painted and scanned in before they landed. I waited to the end of the descent I said 'as it was descending' not 'at the orbit and then descending' they are rearranging the truth. They already know damn well it was done in under 4 minutes that painting and I beat them to the punch with Views that matched their photos taken later. I was not viewing them after they touched down is the important distinction. My Views were in and on record before it reached the surface. I had the picture of the surface where they would land before they got there. And that is the critical distinction. I wasn't painting what they saw I painted what I saw. Before them. They have a video that it took one hour to descend. Big deal. Since I did not take any one hour to paint. I did it as they were just about to touch down it is in my book that I was doing other things. Almost missed it!

Ample proof now exists that it takes less than 4 minutes to do a complete psi unit View. I beat them and got visuals in under 4 minutes. I got the to and from Mars in less time than it takes light to go to and from and that is an undeniable fact. Light takes some 9 plus minutes each way.. I was not painting for any 20 minutes and I certainly did not start as they were at orbit going to descend.

 There are no more view *painters* if they go entirely post material for digital and quantum and further along. Therefore I would think View Paintings are going to be exceedingly rare archaic Art Forms linking to the early Earth. Ancient Pharaohs' Spells. You know in the Bible they fought a Magic War. With the Magicians of Pharaoh being bested in the outcome. You don't just read the bible and play godlet you have to heed the bible. It's instructional. Like a map. Words of prophecy or SpaceTimeLight to guide the way. It is in all reality a way to decoding a Star Trail Map apparently as the 5th D form of greater Reality. We are just learning. Definitely work some ethics. Anyway the overall Chariot Race is on. And it was with Enemies being trampled below and the military in with the fight. With of course always a beginning and an end. Multi directional multi layered.

//I will not be shopping with anyone anytime soon. That's a condition of my reality links. I am in the Time Tunnel. We are not asking we are telling. That's just how it is. About how this works. I am decoding one of many Star Trail Maps the ancients have left us as Star Code apparently. Updates along the trail. Nibbles of the Future bearing standard RV strength, showing in letters, strokes. The ancient forms of writings were strokes. Like key strokes. They used lines and scoops and wedging in wet sand on Earth land. Cuneiform etc. Perhaps there are ways to remove their Spell woven allusions, arrangements, multiplicity layering. In some sense, I do believe we are all being thrown into the midst of their Ancient and very real Magic War. They hunt the Terror Cult and the Bible was on the side of the Egyptians hunting them. If you look in the Bible after they found Moses in the bullrushes. Magic Wars using Battle Spells apparently.

A Remote Viewer is a Spy   Egyptian Hieroglyph for 'Secret'

Seems they are using our outer modern forms to link to the old. While our side seems to be using their ancient shadow View forms. That's interesting. The Cross. It is not Vertical and Horizontal. Maybe that's why they Crucified Christ that way. To rearrange the slant, the form, maybe the Ancient Mayans were indeed right. Check out what Maurice Cotterell found for the corners with the Star mapery imagery; Galaxies and dots visuals and the cross in the corners if you knew to do the correct overlap or overlay. It's fascinating. The Mayan is up. Venus could be connected to the Ben Ben or Benu bird is another form. Space, Flight….imagery and Star Trail Script. And linking as precisely to NOW as an ancient View Theme in its complete Mastery. I am just reporting, decoding, reading the Star Trail. It is already there. The cross was at a 45 degree angle and that's also where Minkowski places his defining lines for the ability to supersede light.

//I like the green blue end of the color spectrum myself. Just personal preference I read once the human eyes are tuning into that end more and more as time goes by. I don't remember what their idea was based on. It was supposedly evolutionary. Red shift blue shift. So spacetime is *not* the way to go inter stellar let alone inter galactic. I got that. If you see it all as one big repeating neckerish 5th quantum there is virtually infinite here/nows. You have to discern a star trail of a linear form. Hence to experience mobility, the overall View Theme of the Chariot, in order to navigate the 5th multi-dimensionality you have to develop a linear Star Trail aimed through the curvature of Space. It is achievable by the sensational 5th. Quantum Psi Viewing is like providing little lights guiding the way. Pointing to the strongest way forwards. Oh so this is now with an Open Stargate on Earth the Earthlings have to earn it. The RV Theme of the Chariot not just War a Race to the Finish. Only one to win, basic Race.

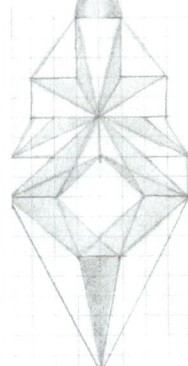

Karnak obelisk for the 'benben: phoenix perched on a mound'; View graphic 1980s
(above) Egyptian Obelisk 'Ben Ben' and phoenix linked; Alexander the Great battle win over Persia, in Iraq, Chariot View linked to current time context as over all View Theme Imagery

Ben Hur? Ben Ben? Get it? The Magic War is a Race to the Finish. (note: in Jihad that translates as Fin-ish, signs fin-ish and surrounding. Their modern approach to Real Time Re invention of the Chariot Race. They are following the Chariot Race like you are following the human race. Convergence? No I am not interested in racing Nasa they cheat. I raced the Rovers and the Lander. They don't. and I won both times. With documentation and Witnesses.

//Well maybe the guys do telekinetic style I am just doing psi chi Viewing I am sensing out the Star Trail. It seems to be definitely that's the points. The ancient 'I Ching' evolved into modern Computers. Literally. Someone gave a copy to a mathematician and he devised the concept. Viewing and prophecy/arking SpaceTimeLight hyper shift quantum leap time tunnel 5th inter-dimensionality are based on computer digital time context to Reveal the whole thing. No computer links no psi links to reveal, they are interwoven as advanced means. There are steps to achieving the Star Trail Outcomes, definitely. The Mayan and Egyptian and others like the Easter Islanders too. With View scripting worked in and showing. Linking as Views and time context precision capable. Merlin did time in a Cave.

Those are respected and best selling modern academic achievements. Skeptics are being ridiculous I am merely adding onto an already established and developed academic trail. This ancient talk of a Time Tunnel and Star Trail are actually very real. Stargate is not just a cutesy name, it's View precision. They already know it is not just pattern recognition. I painted the View of the ground, linked by pixel with dots you haven't lived until you've done that full time for two years. So upon considerable and exacting training to dot to dot eye recognition linking via computer, and a psi talent you learn to be a Viewer. It is totally arduous as a process and entirely engrossing as well. While this training was ongoing, back when I was computer dot linking precisely to Views painted often the day before the unfolding events. Since when you paint it links not just to the Present it also shows links to the other time zones of past and future. I developed a Future Sense. Using the I Ching as a leap platform, basically. I needed some Oracular manner of training my psi to leap ahead and back too, but developing the forward Views. Such is the very real component of Quantum Leap. You get in the Time Tunnel trained as a Leaper and you View not only things in the Now but also in the past and future. It was all entirely proven daily actually it is part of the precognitive characteristic of Viewing. The 5th is time bending to connect in a manner to our now that we can indeed do more than a linear approach to our living. We can manoeuvre in a multi-dimensional fashion.

In terms of normal spatial directions a Viewer can be at times a bit challenged. I do manage travel as an adventure. There are ways to remove the current uses of RNM and subliminals, the Signs they are following, as Spell or Layering. I do believe we are all being thrown into the midst of their Ancient and very real Magic War. They hunt the

Terror Cult and the Bible was on the side of the Egyptians hunting them. If you look in the Bible I have no idea where back when they found Moses in the bullrushes. They had Magic Wars. Wow. Only on Earth. We all got thrown into the midst of a Battle of Spells. For real. Not my 'imagination' at all. Just took a bit of breakthrough examining something. I happen to find Egyptian Hieroglyphs fascinating. One of the many forms of the Uraeus of ancient Egypt is showing on the front of the soldiers helmets, as a shadow form. That likely means the shadows the black and white light extremes of absence of color and full spectrum of color are also included, of course in the Viewing 5th D super wonderland. The Uraeus was ancient Egyptian for 'airet' a rearing Cobra, which shows visually descriptive Eye imagery. The Uraeus shape was found on Pharaoh's crown. Shadow imagery is the descriptive for this time context and the Wizards' horse's name in 'the Lord of the Rings' was Shadowfax. The linkage of the ancient Mayan View themes Star Trail crossed lines and the dots is also found in the ancient Egyptian visual View imagery. They cross over divisions and link to show matching View Themes. And the Star Trail is the same one showing in today's time context link of precision Elsewhere/when. It is the Inter-Stellar and Inter-Galactic Star Code showing the instructional Map in terms of multi dimensional spacetimelight and the 5th. The world is not merely defined linearly as in the realm of spacetime. As the overall View Theme of the Chariot Papyrus describes it is also the 5th enabled curved bow of spacetime and the overall connectiveness of light. The world is multi dimensional as exhibited by the cohesiveness of SpaceTimeLight. Light is intimately connected to spacetime. We leap by a quantum awareness of this and represent our views into the Elsewhere/when of the Time Tunnel by painting holistic capsules of light Views that extend both forwards and backwards in time. In order to appreciate the Chariot Race and the Win by focused aim like the linear arrow of time arching through means of the Quantum Chromo Dynamics of the tension between the arrow on the line and the curve of the bow as it is drawn. So the descriptive of the wonderful View links of the ancient Masterpiece of the Chariot papyrus arrive at our own time context of now. Leaps demonstrated by the computer applications of the here and now modern advancements. I spent over two intensive years linking to computer psi the daily unfolding news events. The training is extremely immersed and entirely rewarding. The pixels of the digital video recordings of events link when you are training, to the direct Views and in a definite precognitive manner. They are painted a day ahead of a lot of the digitally confirmed precision views. Indeed it was the means of the computer confirmation and a first ever never before done, Nasa launch with a camera that allowed a backwards view of the receding earth's ground visuals linking to a View from a preceding day that actually confirmed it was beyond doubt the View having precognitive as in knowing the future ahead of time, that was involved in Viewing. The Minkowski's 4d as 2d enabling a visual representation of a $v>c$ effect in respect to multi levelled events and timelines. We can cross over to see the 5th multi dimensionality by using the shift ability of time moving both forwards and backwards not just in a forwards manner. Quantum science has already well established this with the appropriate diagrams. Of course the time context of now comes into play with the Stargate View theme Inter-Stellar Star Trail visuals linking with today's historical reference of the Attica Prison Riot photos of 1971. Here the bat and cross one physical object being the bat and one visual sign the cross. The bat and cross are linked to the ancient Egyptian hieroglyphic as well.

1. View match confirming Precognition; NASA launch first time camera taking ground visuals 2. Bow & Arrow of linear Time through Curved SpaceTimeLight ; note 45 degree angle of arrow, 2D of 4D v>c, with the bow lines describing the 90 degree angle (a complete Z with another base line parallel to the arrow, running in the opposite direction, from end point to zero-point/Axis); glyph markers for lord, heart/waves, infinity and merlin, psi energy/spacetimelight 5th D)

Described as 'hem neter' showing the crossed over means of reading to translate that combination. Here it is showing up as a timely View focus in photos of a past event. Linked in relevant significance to today in that it specifically shows up as a recognizable pattern, the Star Trail, security and the dot to dot aspect for not only points to decode but also to form a spacetime linear connection from one point to another. In effect we receive timely information on a similar path. Spacetimelight links often repeat to link over times, past to now, and now to future. And here is an example of the past as in both the ancient Mayan and Egyptian to link as Star Trail Cross visuals. Leaping via Quantum 5th to the Knights with swords. The heavy swords were indeed carried on the backs of horses and represent markers to connect the Swords on the survival Star Trail What if big scary aliens came dripping acid in through the door. Sure, I would get over it real fast. But the rest of the time I would likely just perfer to deter them and not kill them. I would get things changed first. I am not out for any miss rambo. I am not into it, I am a Viewer but I still manage to put up with the hostiles on Earth. This is Earth. It is not Utopia. And who says Aliens don't eat people? You need to rethink your list of what's the worst potentials under modern quantum conditions. That's what I think.

That's a scary one two they're here and you have the RNM weapons operating. It's not Inter-Galactic crime to you? It just seems to me it would be. They don't want Sharia and Jihad stepping onto Space Platforms with 5th Hypershift capabilities. So, it's a bit much to think any Alien form would be just automatically be 'coming to make friends with gifts and welcome' at this point. Another Keanu-esque hey folks there is a Quantum Matrix running concurrently with daily reality- moment.

The hyper shift phenomenon, Quantum viewing. It is what we do here. If you don't mind. I sure do a mean Amazon Blow Gun Dart. In Blue. And natural. Pigeon math but that's what it is. Don't be absurd it is a reflection using paint, very effects and tension oriented it is called technically, Quantum Chromo Dynamics that is what it is known as. It is a specialization. I am a specialist. That's a decent blow gun dart it is a psi descriptive unit you have to learn how to see them. It's like a fine art that way, in its visuals, to develop the appreciation for them. It has it's moments. All art forms do really. This is a psi quantum creative expressive form of art. Using painting and writing, poetry, canvases, other medium like audio/video movies etc. our creative art is linking to the strongest Star Trail indications. As would be expected. This Psychic Art form or Oracle for prophecy is based on the multi layered and directional hyper shift phenomenon. It's a science art psychic chi combination. Therefore, the 5th SpaceTimeLight is as currently established via psi Viewing which has a velocity greater than the speed of light. Where $v > c$ or more precisely, $V (Psi) > c$, however it is still an indication that the speed barrier of light can indeed be broken. The ultimate limit passed as exhibited by the Race with the Phoenix. I had a fax window pop up on my computer every day when I clicked on the Cruise Jewel Box Constellation window, at jpl.nasa.gov for over 3 years. I stopped over religious/political persecution, Slavery and false imprisonment in violation of my civil liberties. No time off, held under RNM abuse. Appropriate piece of serendipity, note the Pirates' eye patch visual shape! (In the white dot outlined 'face' shape at bottom right, is a black eye patch shape.)

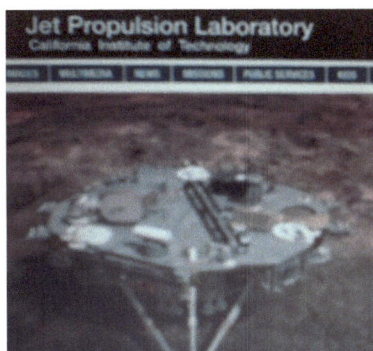

JPL Phoenix Mars Lander; excerpt enlarged 'Pirates' eyepatch shape inside dot outline.

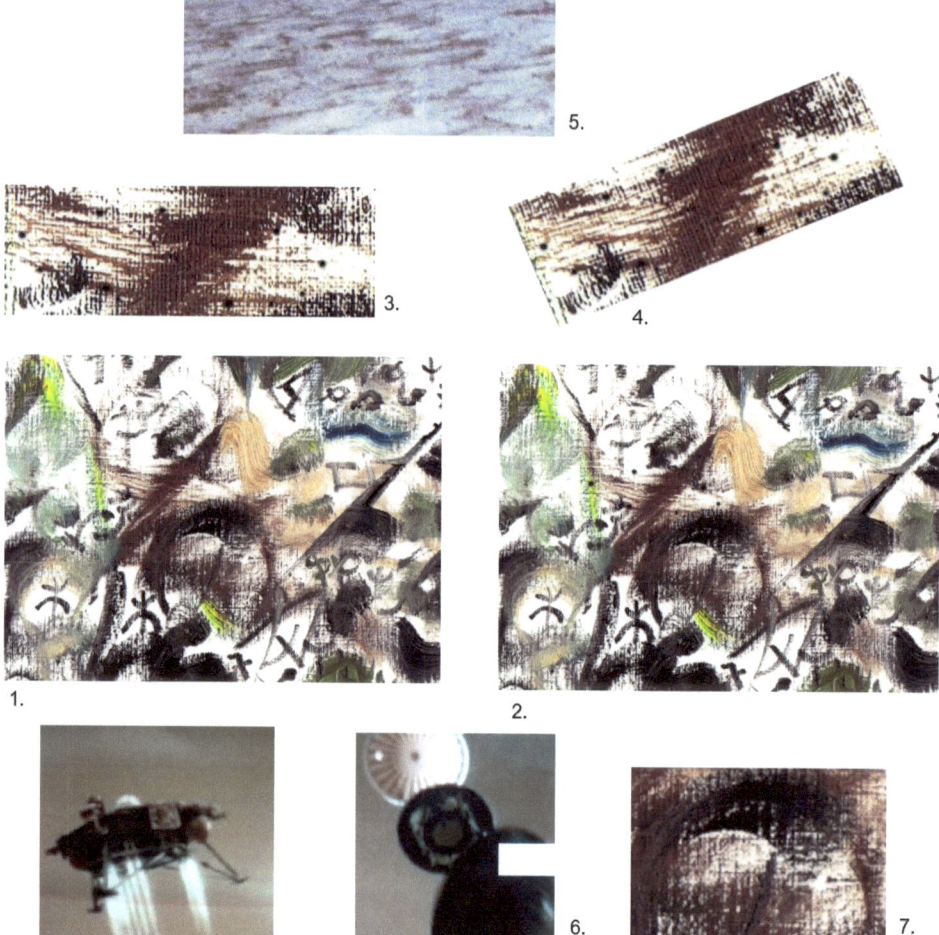

1. Original Mars Phoenix Lander VIEW painting done in a complete psi packet in under 4 minutes the day it was descending to the surface, as they were approaching the final touchdown.

Many witnesses and confirmed facts. 2. Surface match outlined in dots, as shown in the excerpt above as 3. And 4. With dots outlining it as turned to match the angle of the subsequent photos taken of the surface area where the Phoenix landed, 5. So it is easier for you to see the match up with the lines the color visuals are in the book 'Remote Viewing: Knights of Mars' page 177.

6. Is the Phoenix Lander pictures by Nasa of the lander and its parachute and 7. Is the View of the chute as it was opened and descending. See the book mentioned for the 'ICE' View paint too.

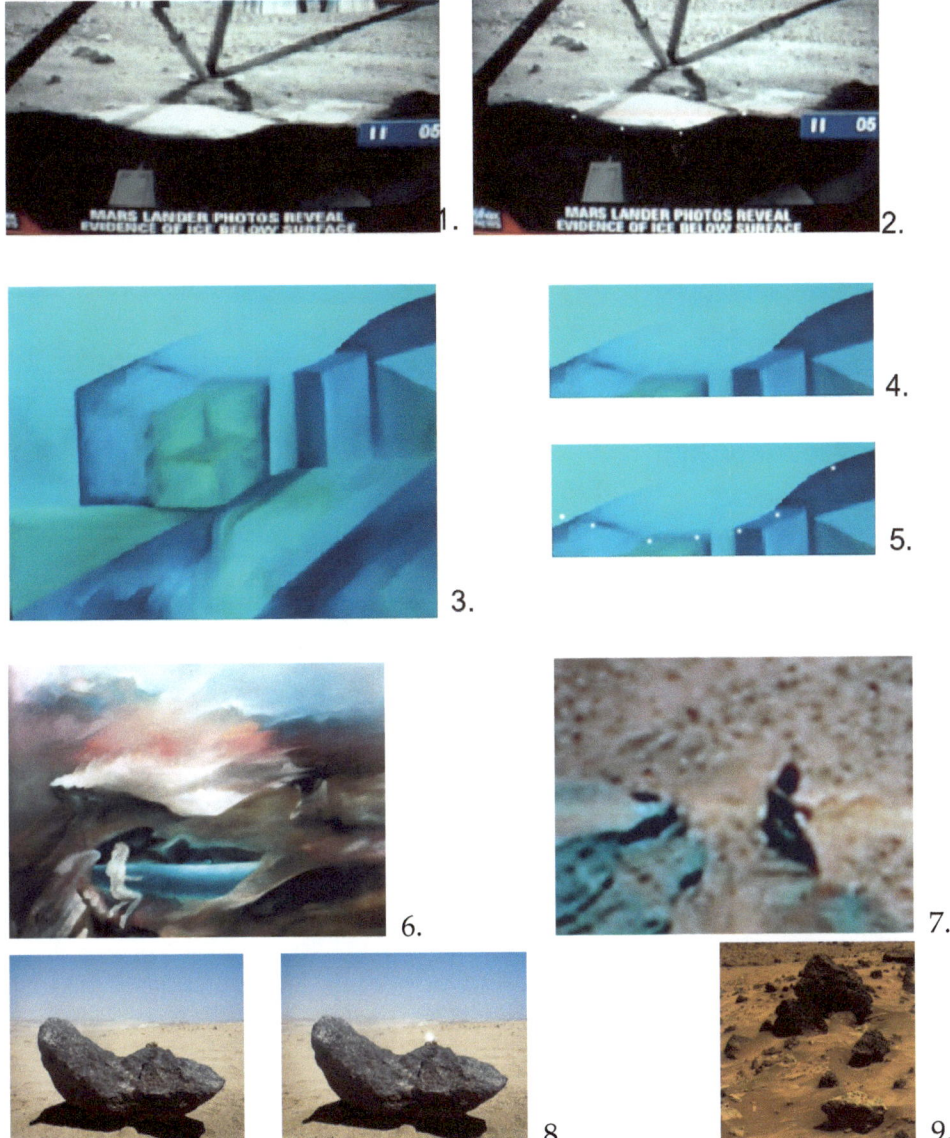

1. Photo of ground immediately under the Phoenix Lander on Mars
2. Same photo with dots outlining the portion that matches in the older View paint 'Ice'
3. Older VIEW painting 'Ice'
4. Top right corner from 'Ice' match to ice patch under Phoenix Lander on Mars surface.
5. Match outlined in white dots for ease of identifying.
6. Older VIEW painting of 'Girl with Pink Sky'.
7. Surface photo of unusual rock arrangement on Mars, match to the older View painting.
8. Rocks on Mars showing similar overlap illusion, just created by distance with the one in the foreground overlapping the one in the background.
9. Rocks on Mars, likely meteorites, same rough granular surfaces as the 'girl' image.

On the surface of Mars, last but not least, the tiny patches of frozen water ice found by the Phoenix Lander in a visual shape linked to one the ancient Egyptian Master Viewers accomplished before. With a Hieroglyph that matches and meant 'God' with the phonetics 'neter' and the determinative being a single stroke to show one, as in one God. So, you see God has already laid official claim to the Planets of Sol, and left suitable flag markers for us to learn this magnificent fact. That is called proof, and v>c with SpaceTimeLight bent like a bow. Quantum psi 5th D leaps which are abundantly viable and thoroughly astounding.

   neter = God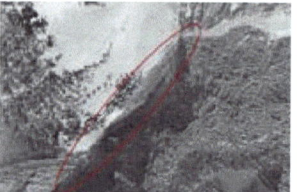

1. Patches of ice found near Phoenix Lander, match to Egyptian hieroglyph 'neter' flag

2. Remote View 2006, Noah's Ark far right in painting, 3. match to CIA photo of Ark; 4. match also to the Afghanistan long grey streak visual descriptive of the Helicopter; ie: overlapping View themes within one time context of Viewing in a single RV painting

You take about two years to learn View language. I findit is an ongoing process. The wee boat diagram above it distinguishes it as a multi connected time event visual link. The View links to more than one 'event' and they are not linked themselves in terms of actual influence. There is not immediate kinetic event of any substantial or measurable manner. Nothing was 'changed' by the observation. The same way video footage does not directly influence our reality structure. We do not 'make or interfere' with reality and natural events by making video movies. Same deal here. Proven by the fact there are no things moving around using our normal optical channels and this is using the same optical channels. I am not sitting here smelling views. These are light connected and that is as inseparable from spacetime as our vision is to the eye, the optics system.

Laser holograms are similarly linked to the light and visual process.

So far as modern upgraded understanding of reality. A Quantum Psi link is a co-author. And we did do it together every step of the way. That's current state of reality, also known as the comprehensive truth.

Go back again to the Knights' times. Crusaders with swords on horses, also concerned with security, to again Leap forwards to today's links to the horse in the field with the leg patterns matching one of the ancient Egyptian Hieroglyphs for Mer, the same angled lines. Then the Crusader View theme the Crosses with the Inter Stellar Stargate visuals, the dots, orbs and orbits visuals, linking forwards to the current discussion of an Open Stargate with its Star Trail instructional Map.

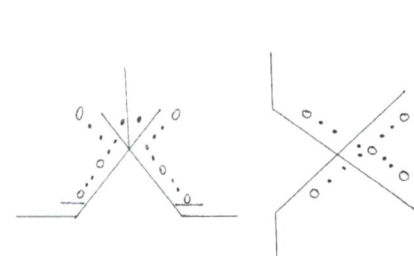

Mayan Star Trail visuals of a Cross linking to the ancient Egyptian as well, (above) relevant parts redrawn, according to the 'Mayan Prophecies' by Maurice Cotterell & Adrian Gilbert; (below left) excerpt from Egyptian Hieroglyph under it, in full, showing the spiral and dot/orb inter-stellar Map descriptive match; (below right) neter=flag cross reading descriptive phonetically speaking and placing the LORD first as the meaning of the visual representation accordingly; (right) View painting 2003 with cross lines descriptive

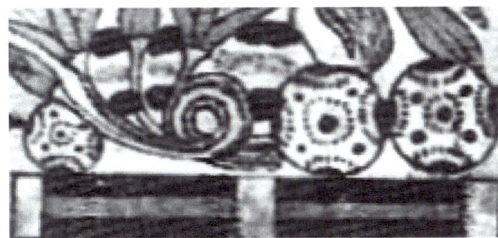

Excerpt - Egyptian Hieroglyphs; 'hem neter' flag=God object=Servant, so 'servant of God'; Mayan glyph

(above) Egyptian View encapsulation; *Teleportation booths?* bottom row; bottom right corner enlarged; matching tire marks by US LA cops during a chase, (below) speeds up to 110 mph; 1971 Attica prison riot with Viewed bat and cross

Afghanistan 2009 Col. Oliver North (Fox News)

 m : IN

The Wizard is IN

 Mer  Mer 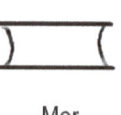 Mer

'FAST' special ops, Afghanistan 2009 dawn raid on drug compound, accompanied by Col. Oliver North of Fox News; in my written RV I got the wall, number 11 on the arm patch, the dog on a leash, the ground stalks and other links established by Remote Viewing; they were on a roll, they did another pre-dawn DEA, Nato Special Ops, Afghan Cops, Raid of more junkie fields

 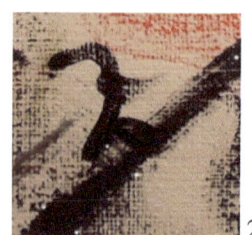

1. gun part soldier in Afghan; 2. view match to gun part; 3. ancient Remote Viewing architecture in Iran, Naqsh-e-Rostam RV match to desktop computers as well as ie: guns and ammunition visuals like in 4 and below; excerpt from Egyptian Hieroglyphics (far bottom right)

Dog RV

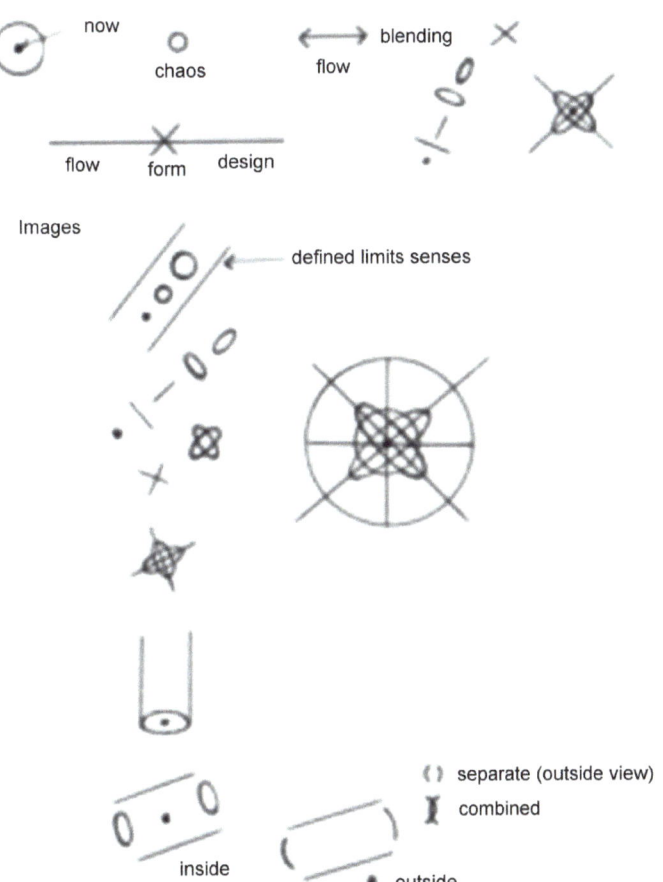

graphic 'pc compatible' (desktop pc)

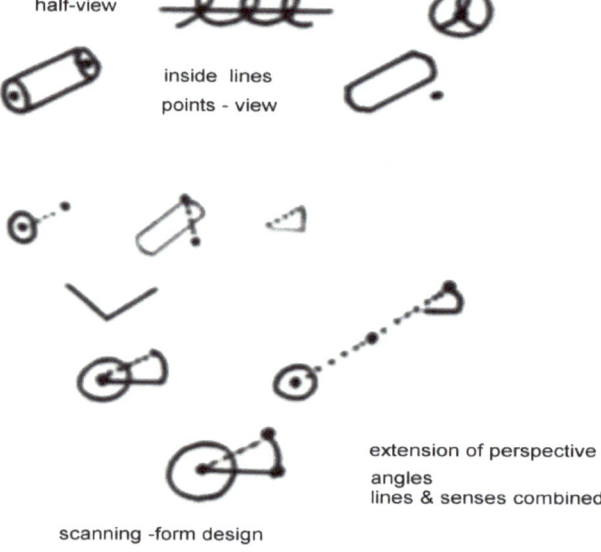

scanning -form design
-sense of scanning leads to focusing
-sense of design leads to direction

'Frog Ship' View oil/canvas painting '95

August 5th, 1983

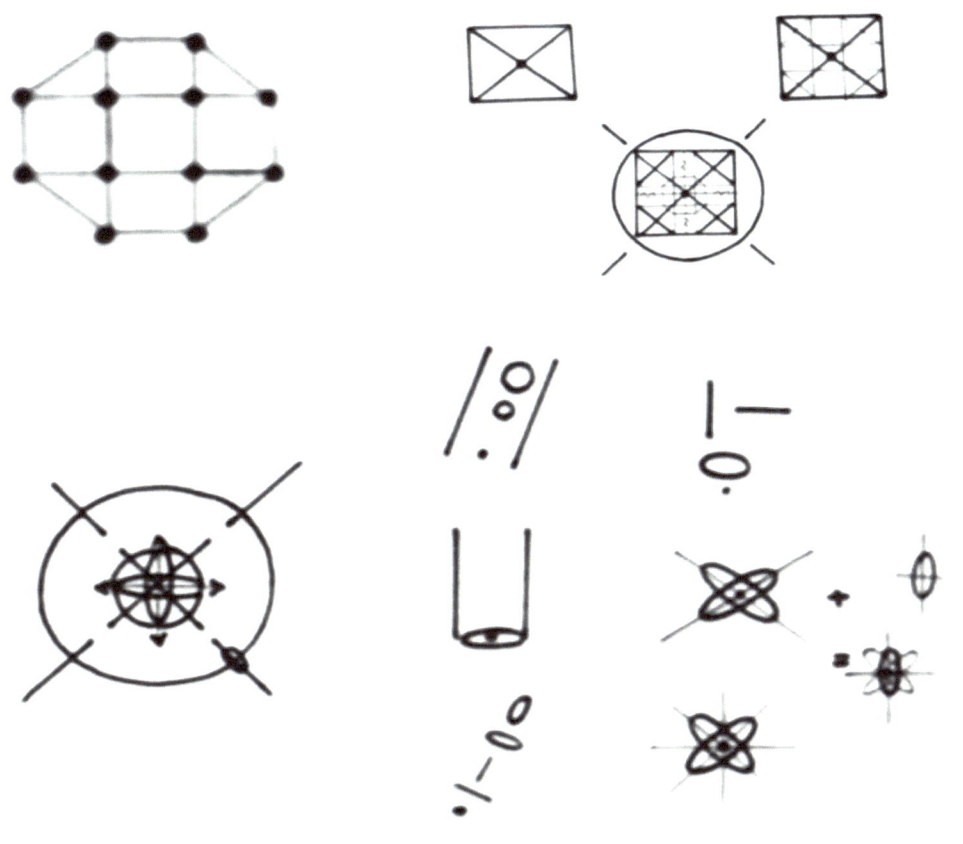

'Dino round up Ship' View oil 1996

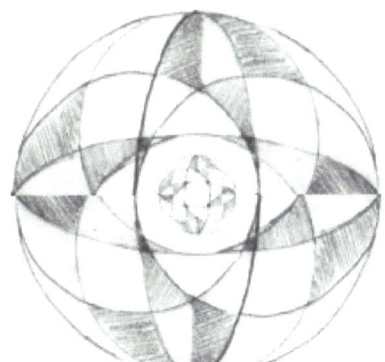

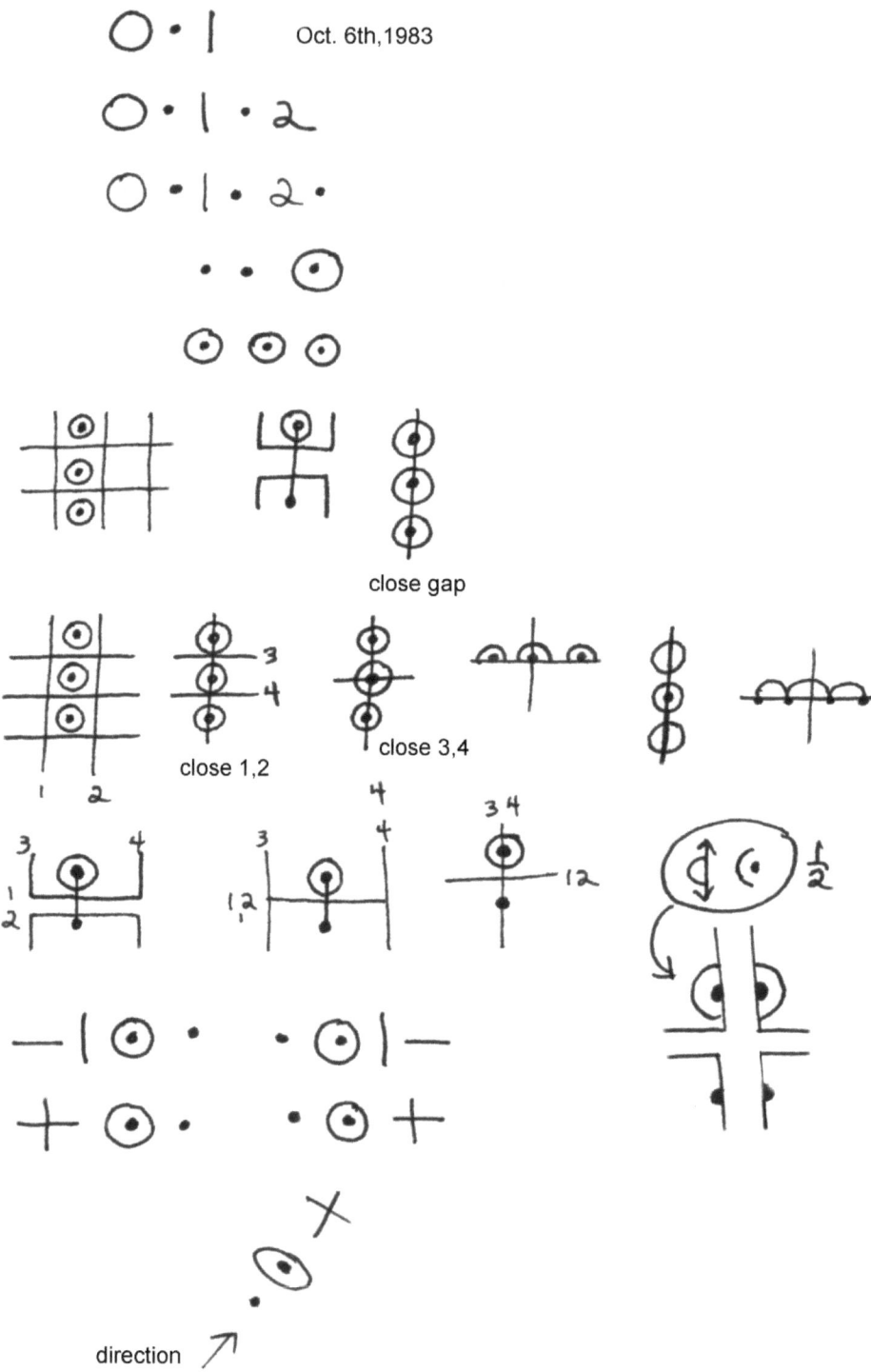

Oct. 6th, 1983

close gap

close 1,2

close 3,4

direction

Star Script — First Viewer 5th D

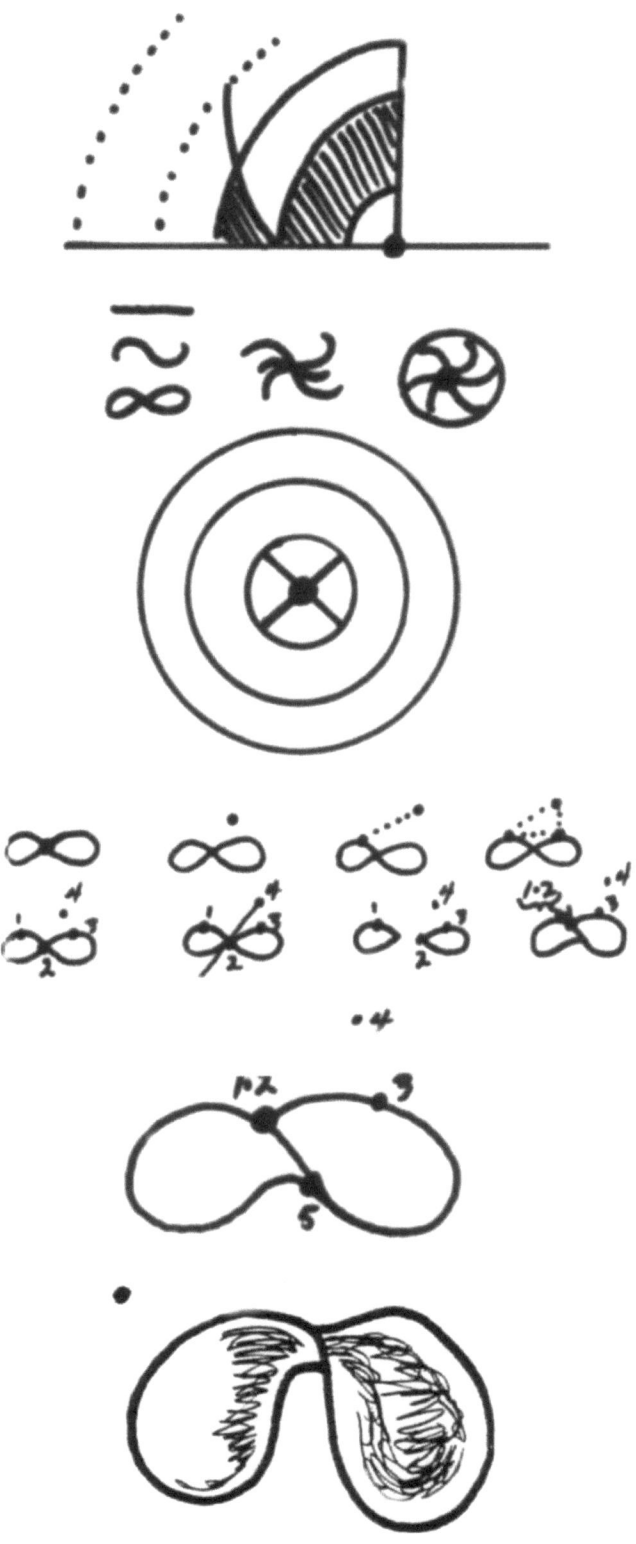

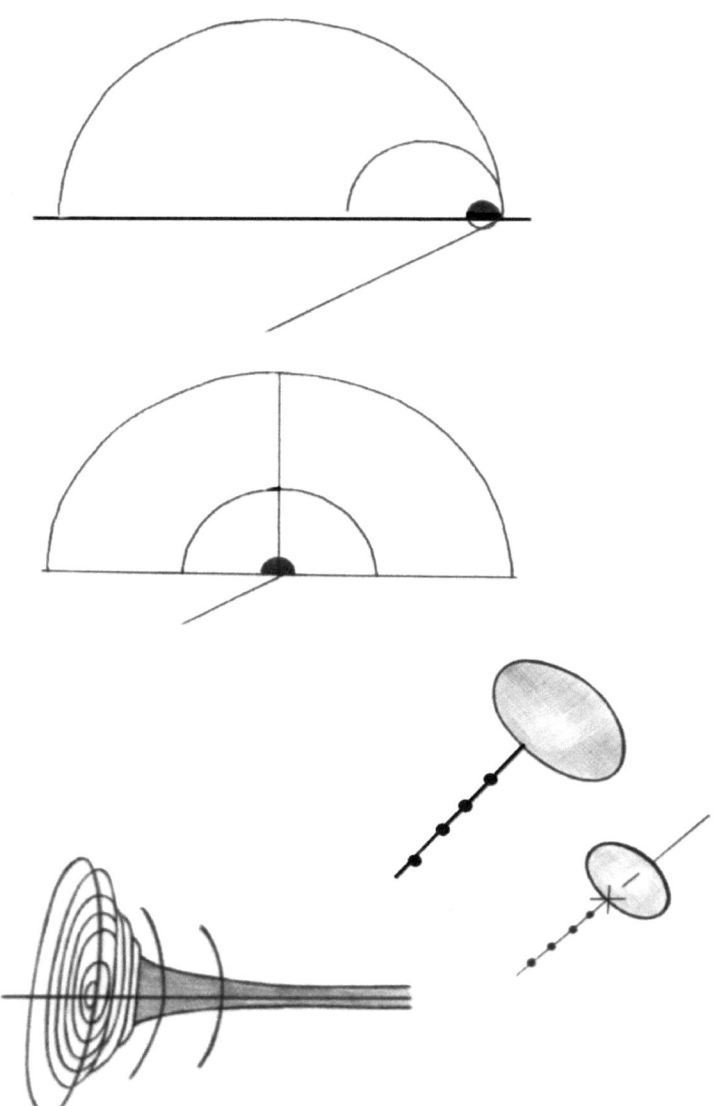

Star Script — First Viewer 5th D

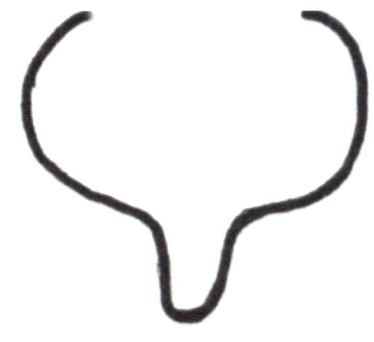

'Mathland' View paint 2005

 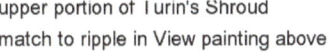
upper portion of Turin's Shroud
match to ripple in View painting above

Soldier's rifle butt shape match to RV Afghan. '09

 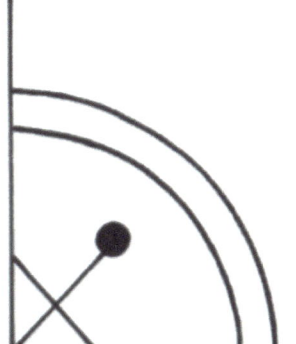

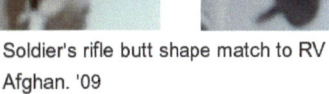
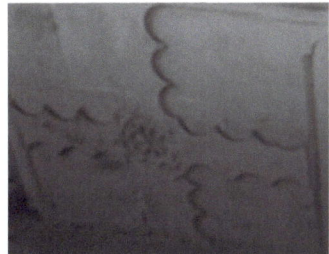
Roslyn Chapel

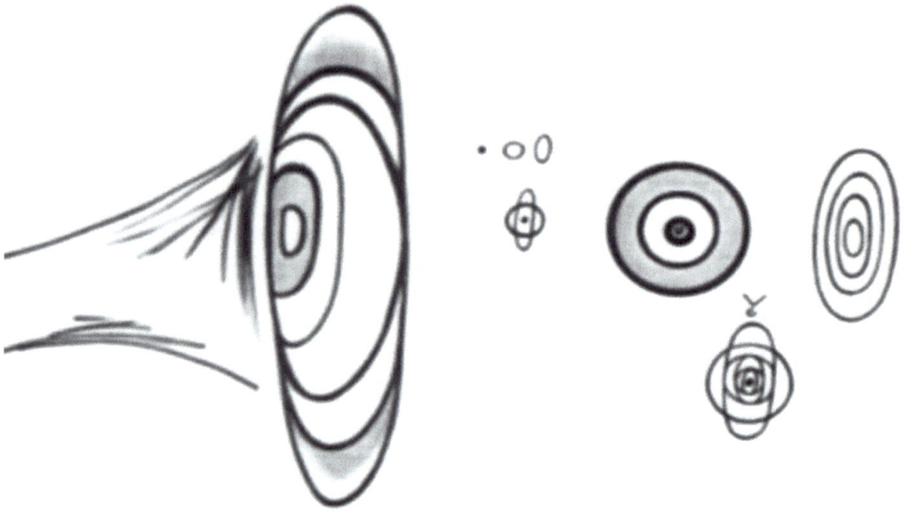

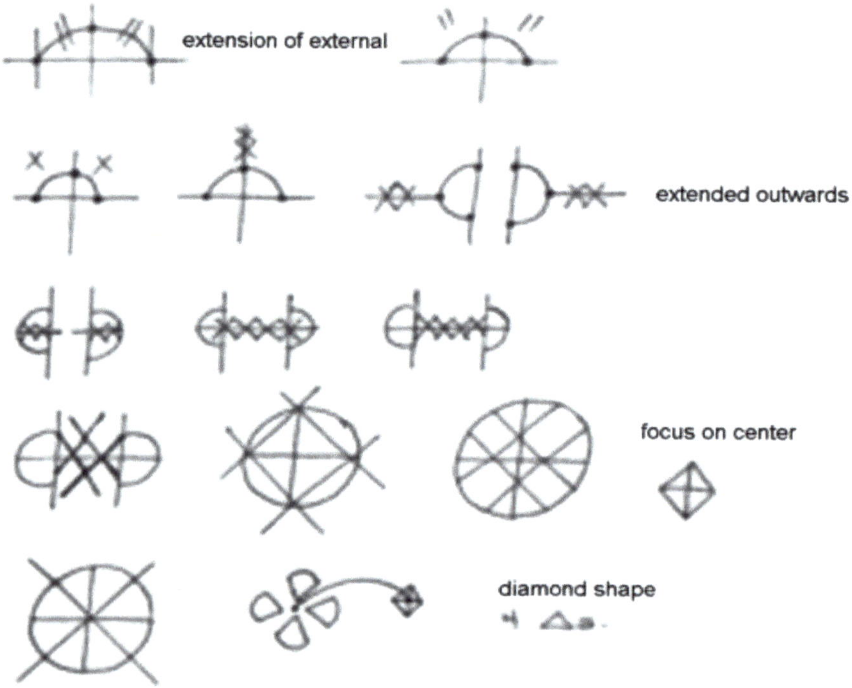

Star Script — First Viewer 5th D

extension of external

extended outwards

focus on center

diamond shape

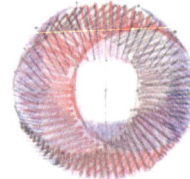
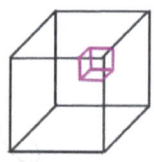

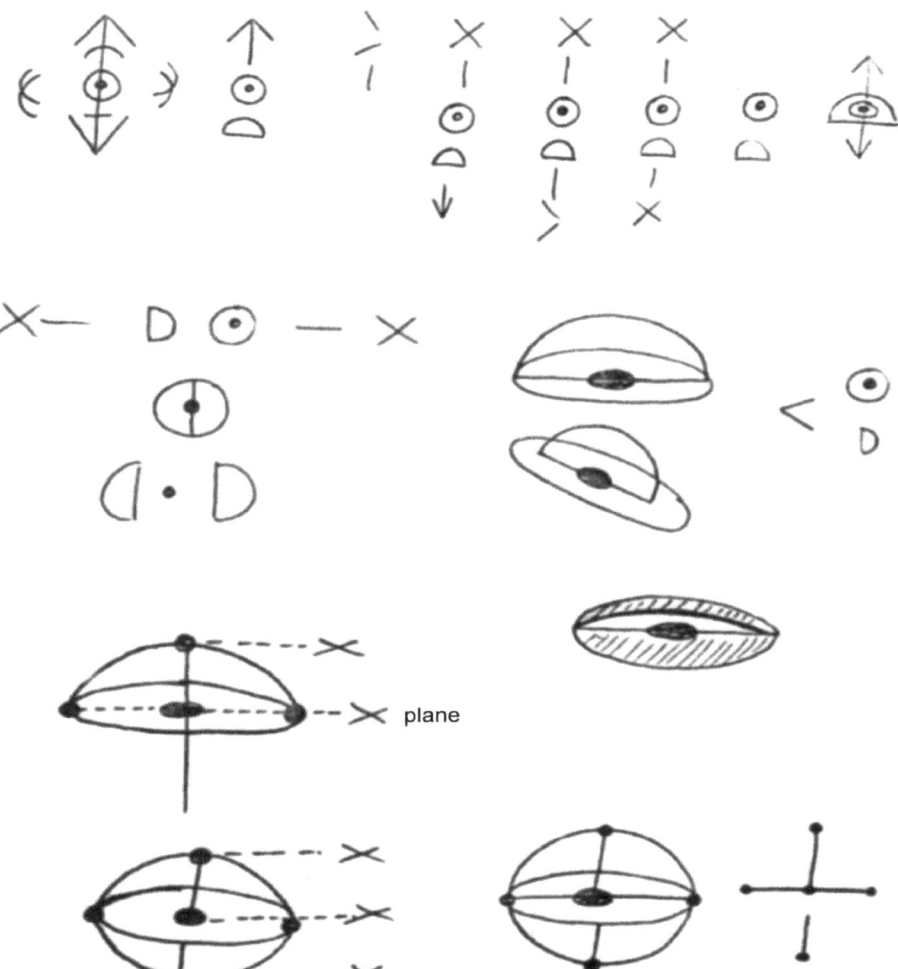
Sept. 16, 1983

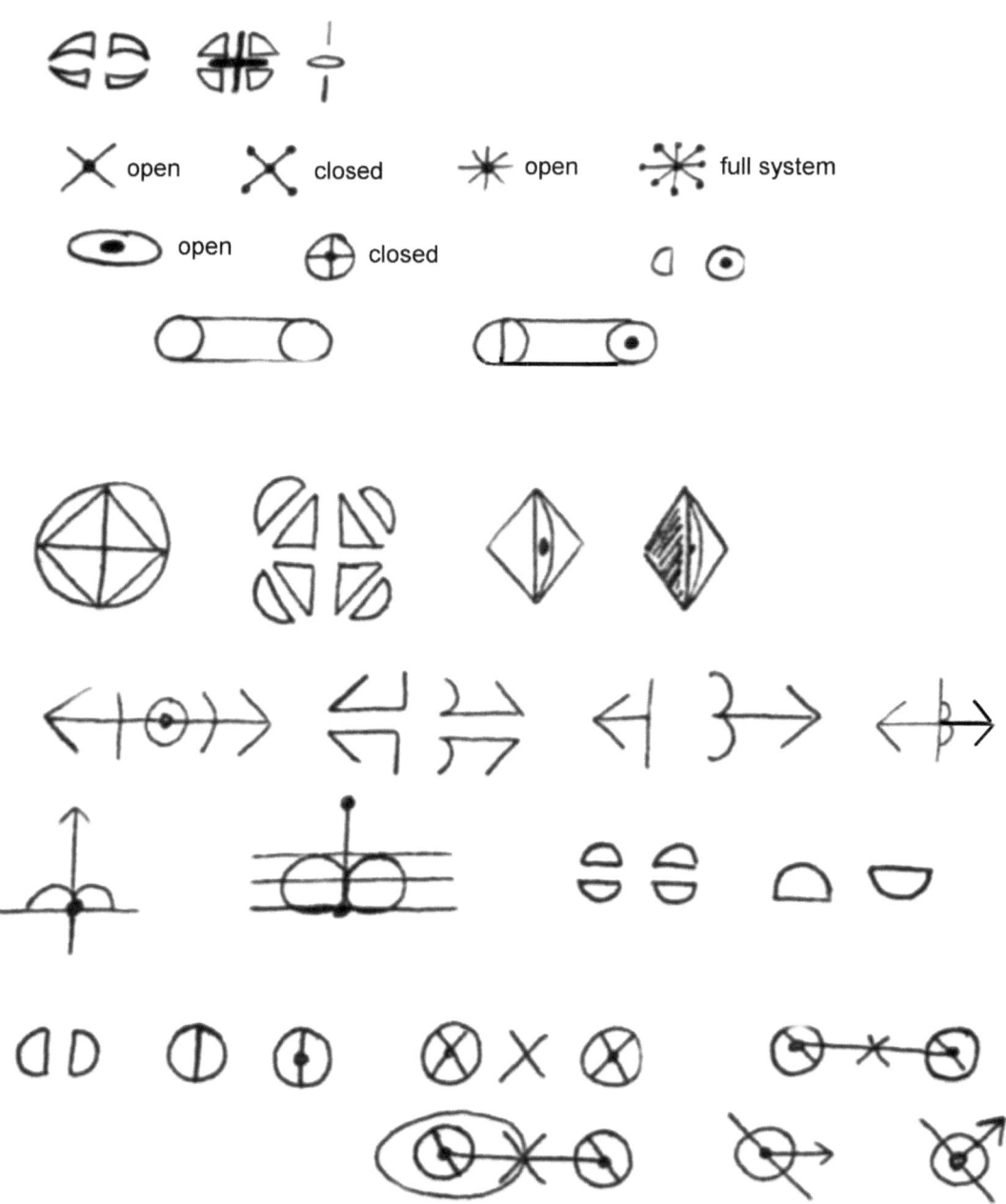

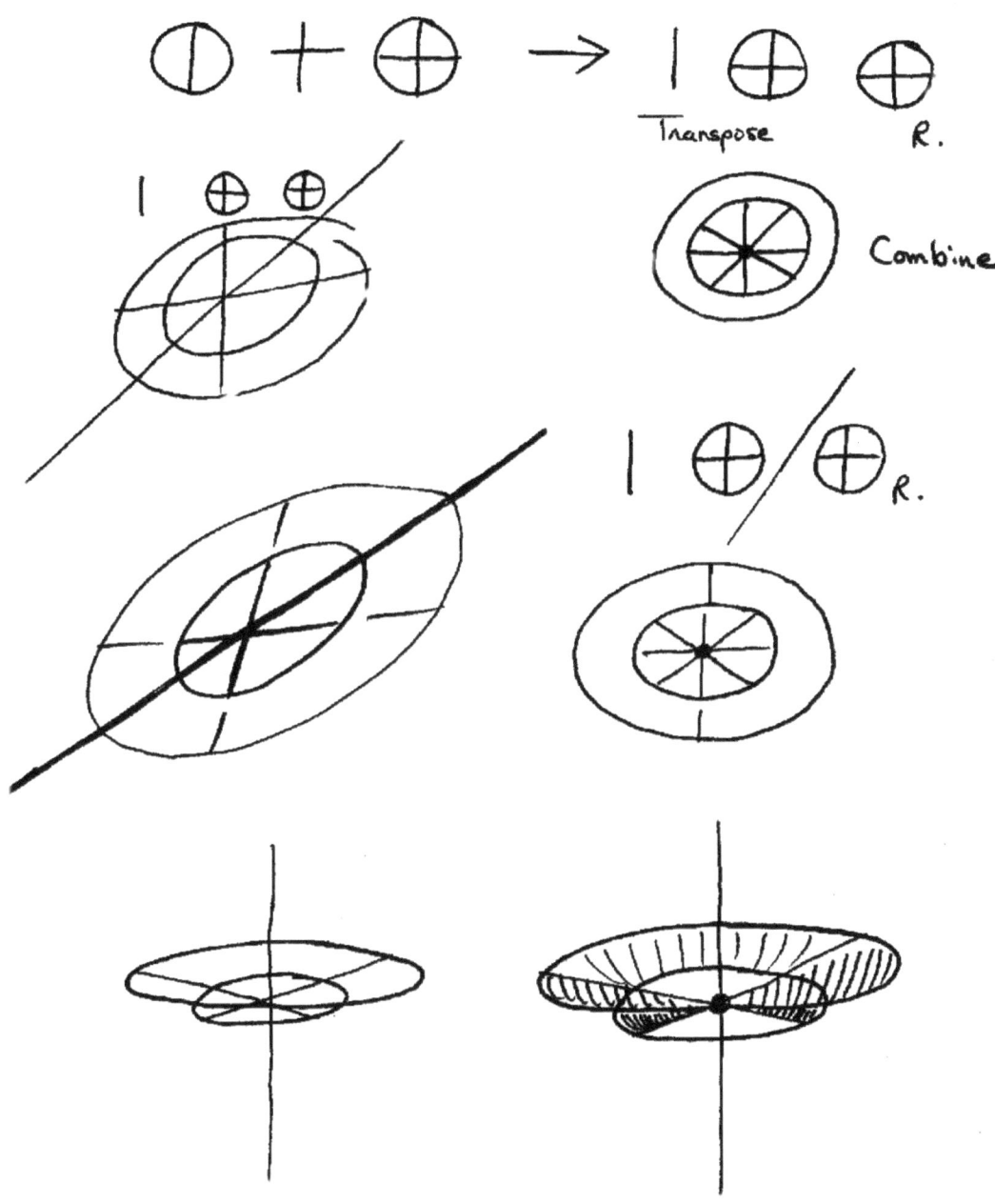

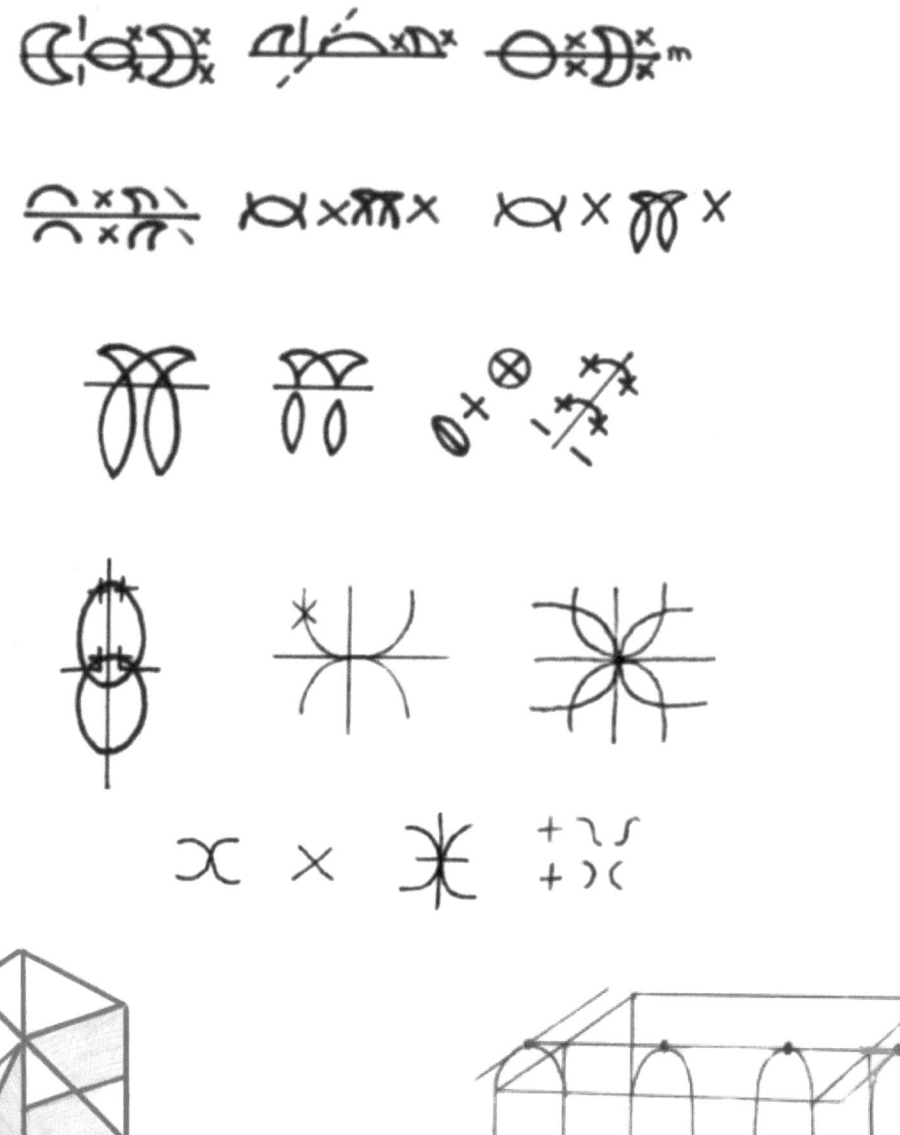

August 7th, 1983

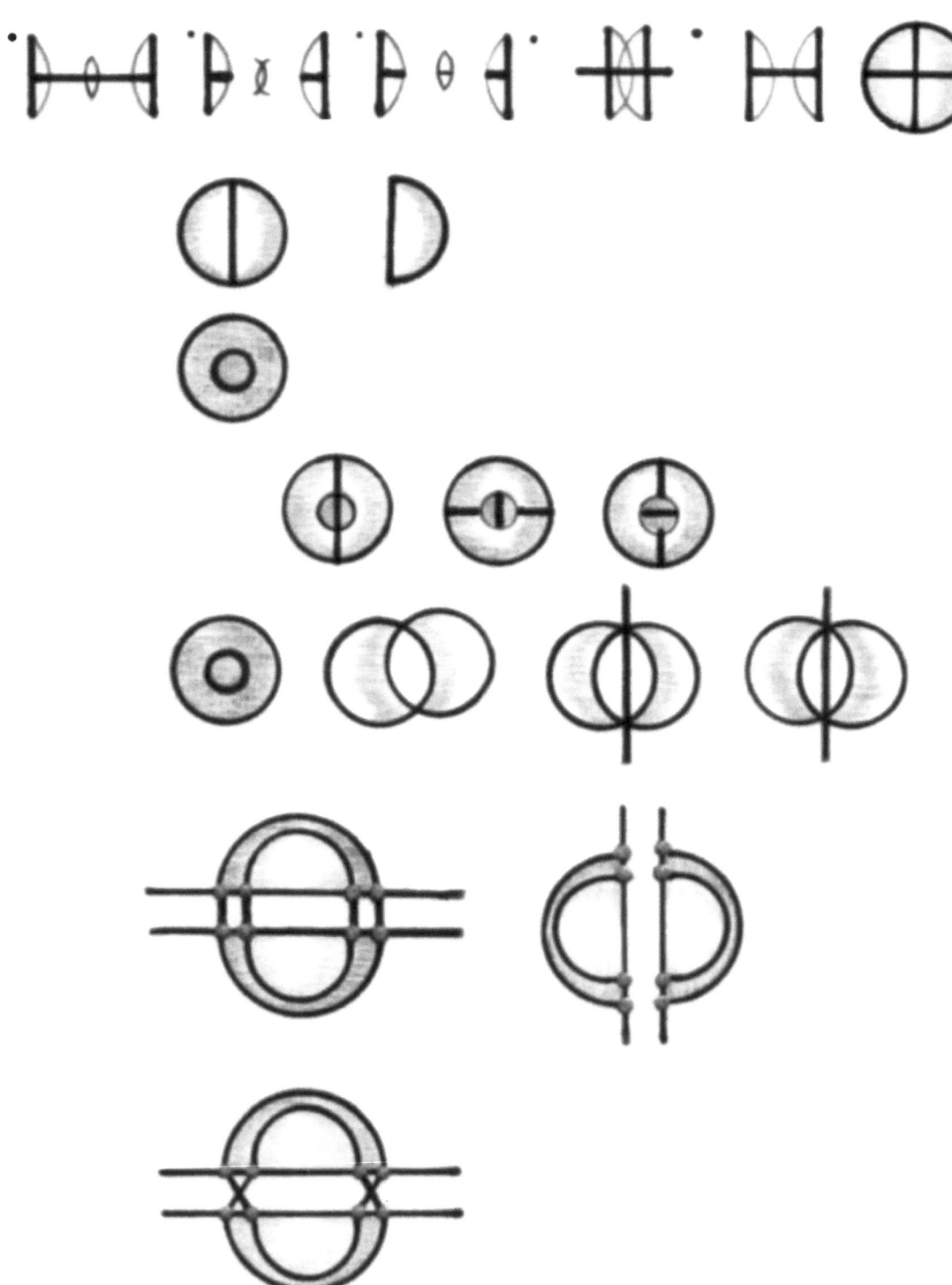

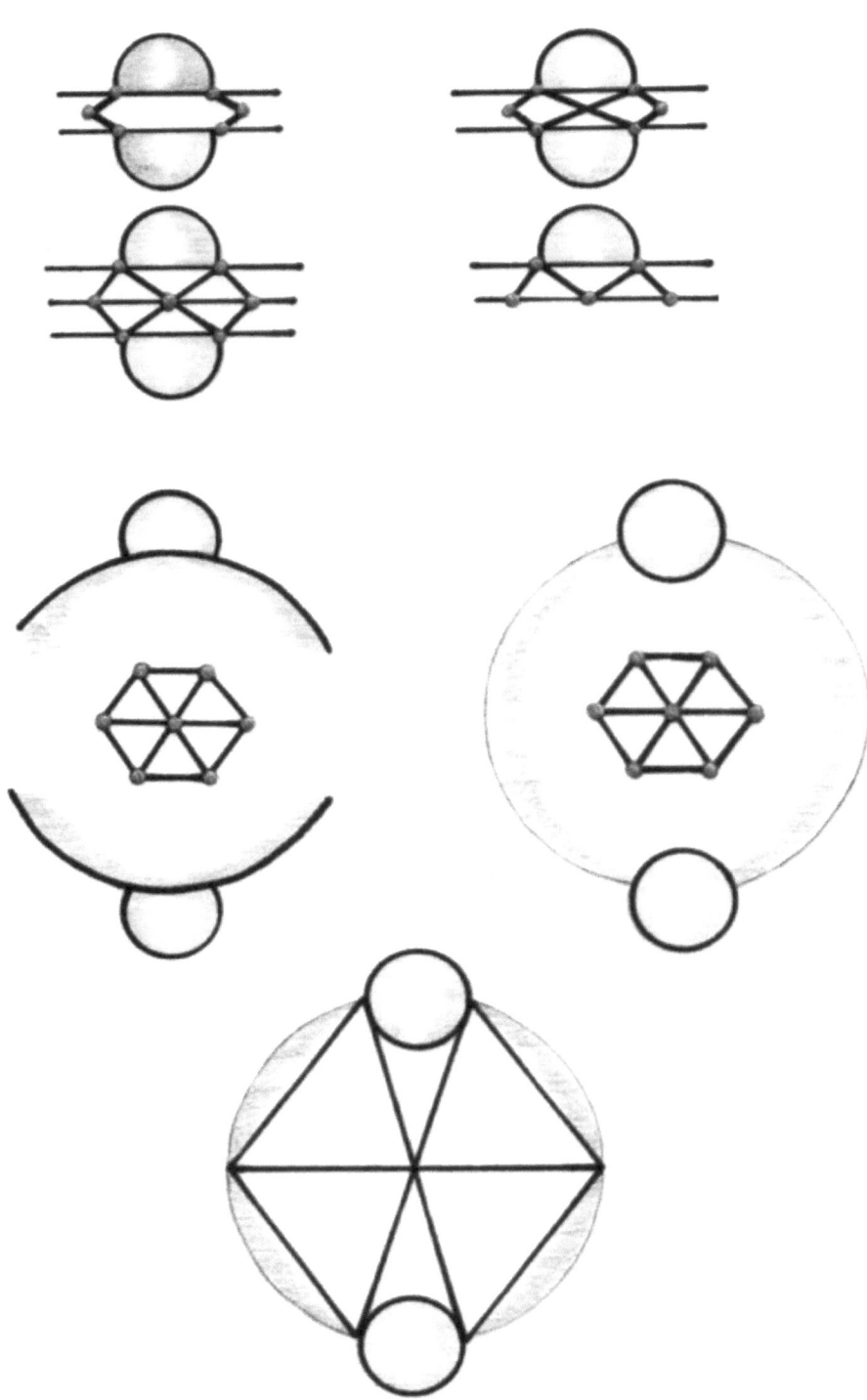

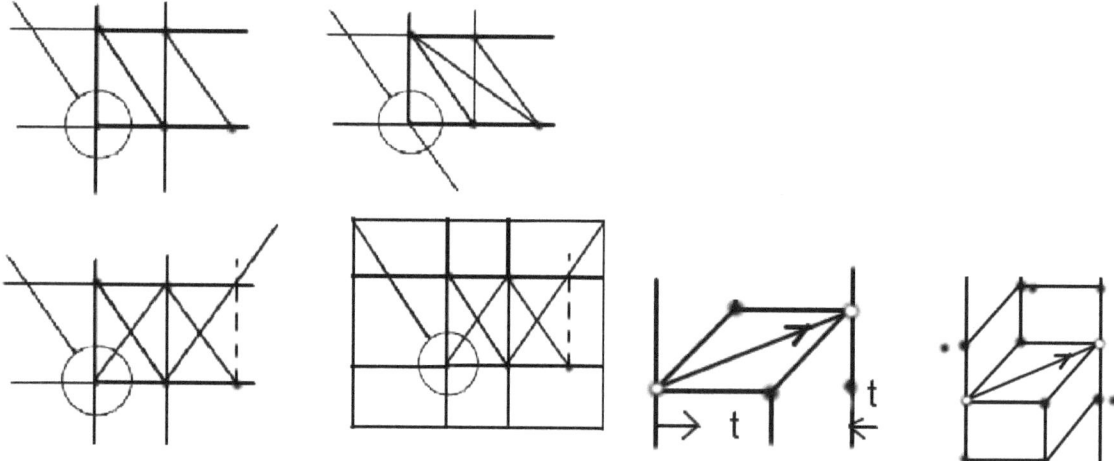

Diagrams illustrating tangent, gap, extension, parallel and diagonal, limitation frame or field range (multi-dimensional inclusive), and 5th D leap dynamics. Descriptive of Remote Viewing techniques, used to provide visuals. Accompanied of course, by a psi directed empathic sense. And guided by a strong sense of instincts developed to ensure survival.

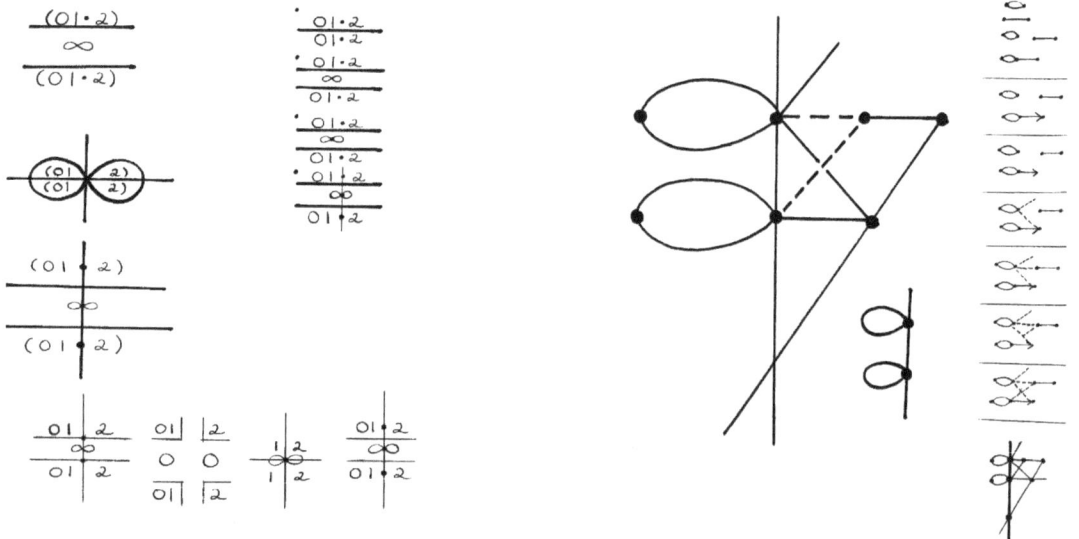

Star Script — First Viewer 5th D

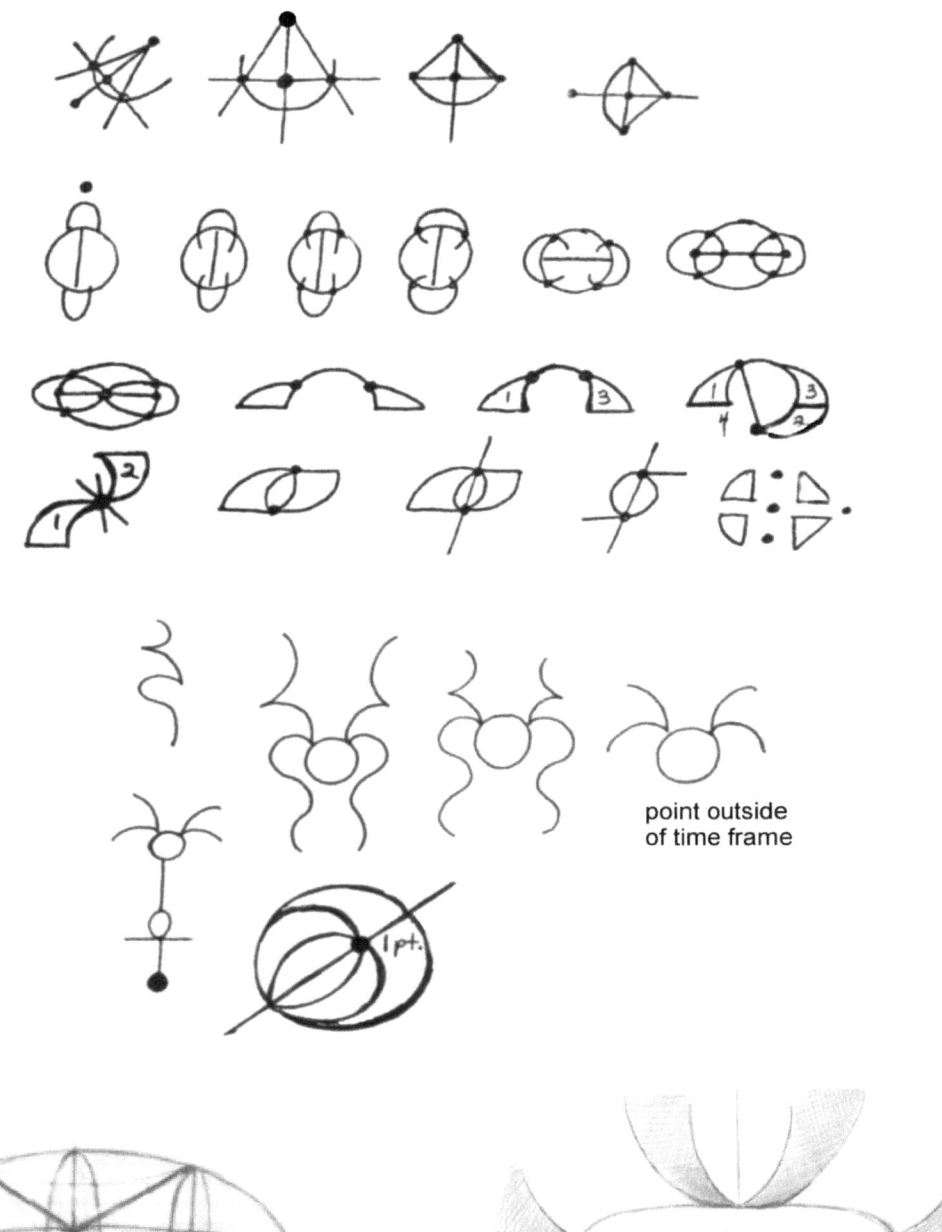

point outside of time frame

Star Script — First Viewer 5th D

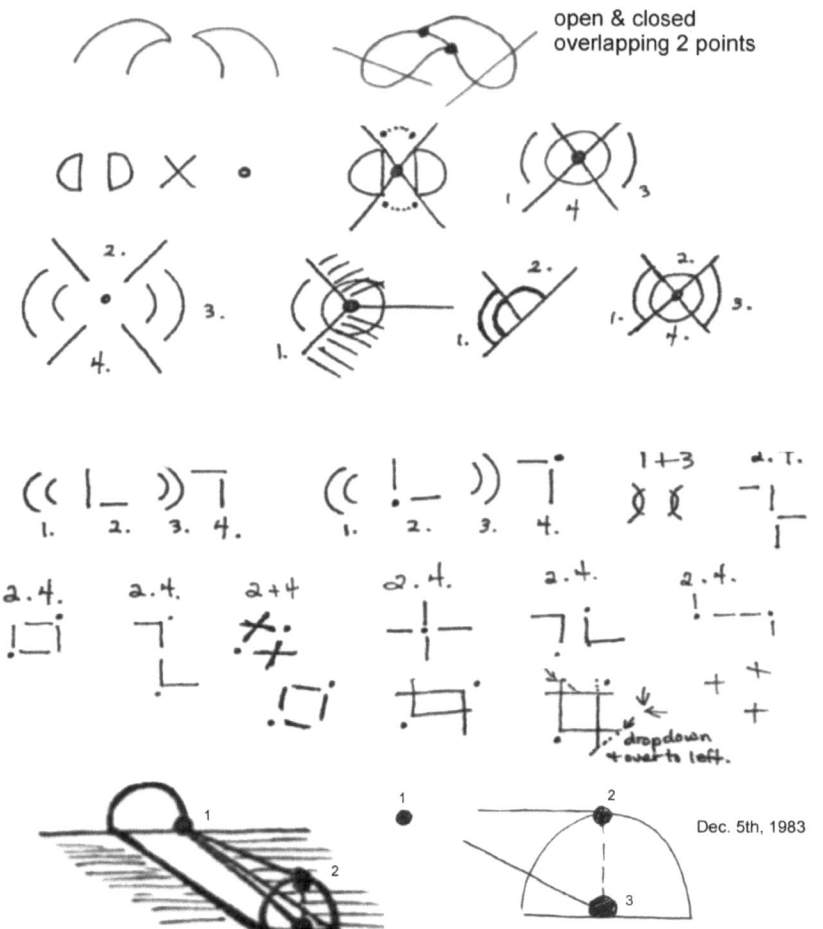

Dec. 5th, 1983

Mysterious white substance found around Mars; glows in dark
NASA Rover photo Sol 691 from raw footage online
Just don't click on any mysterious faxes while you're there if you go online….they 'recruit' psychics straight to ye olde Space Bugs Mind Farms….er, Reconnaissance. They only pay them if they have University Degrees and hang in their elite circles. Otherwise, it's the old Slavery routine. Seriously. We here at Stargate like to warn other Earthlings. And Deepside aliens too, if any come along.

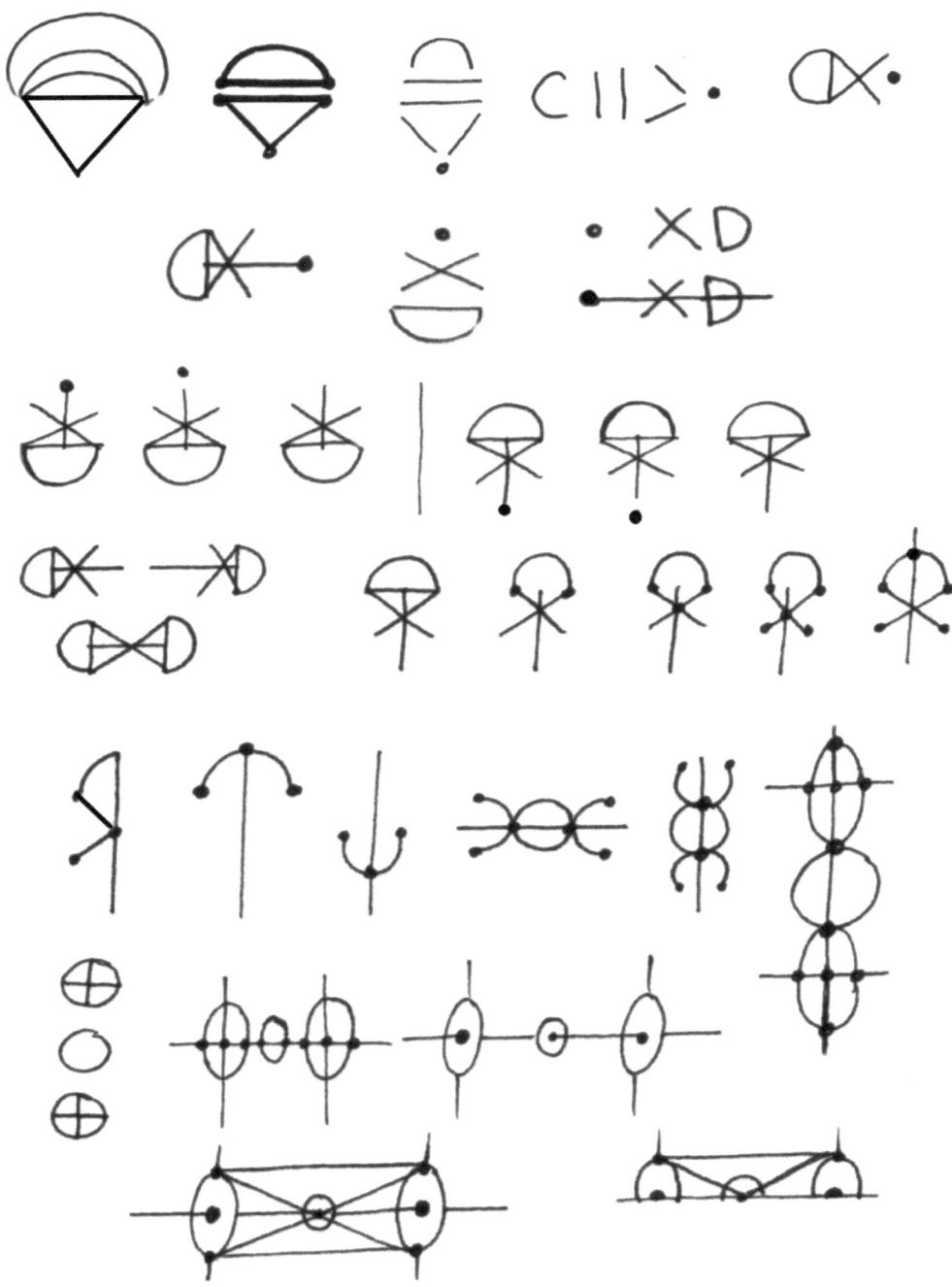

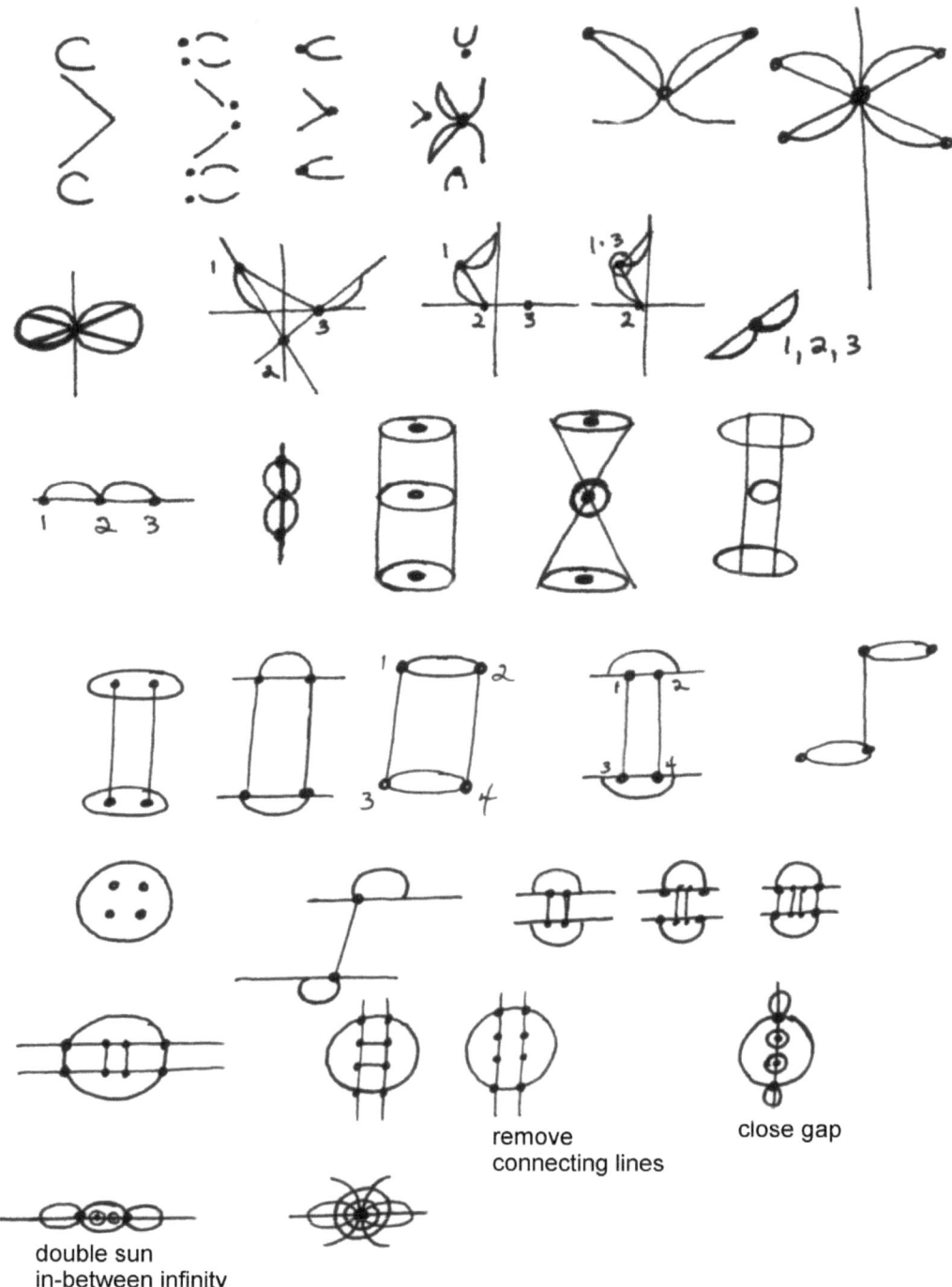

remove
connecting lines

close gap

double sun
in-between infinity

• defining Area of a Plane

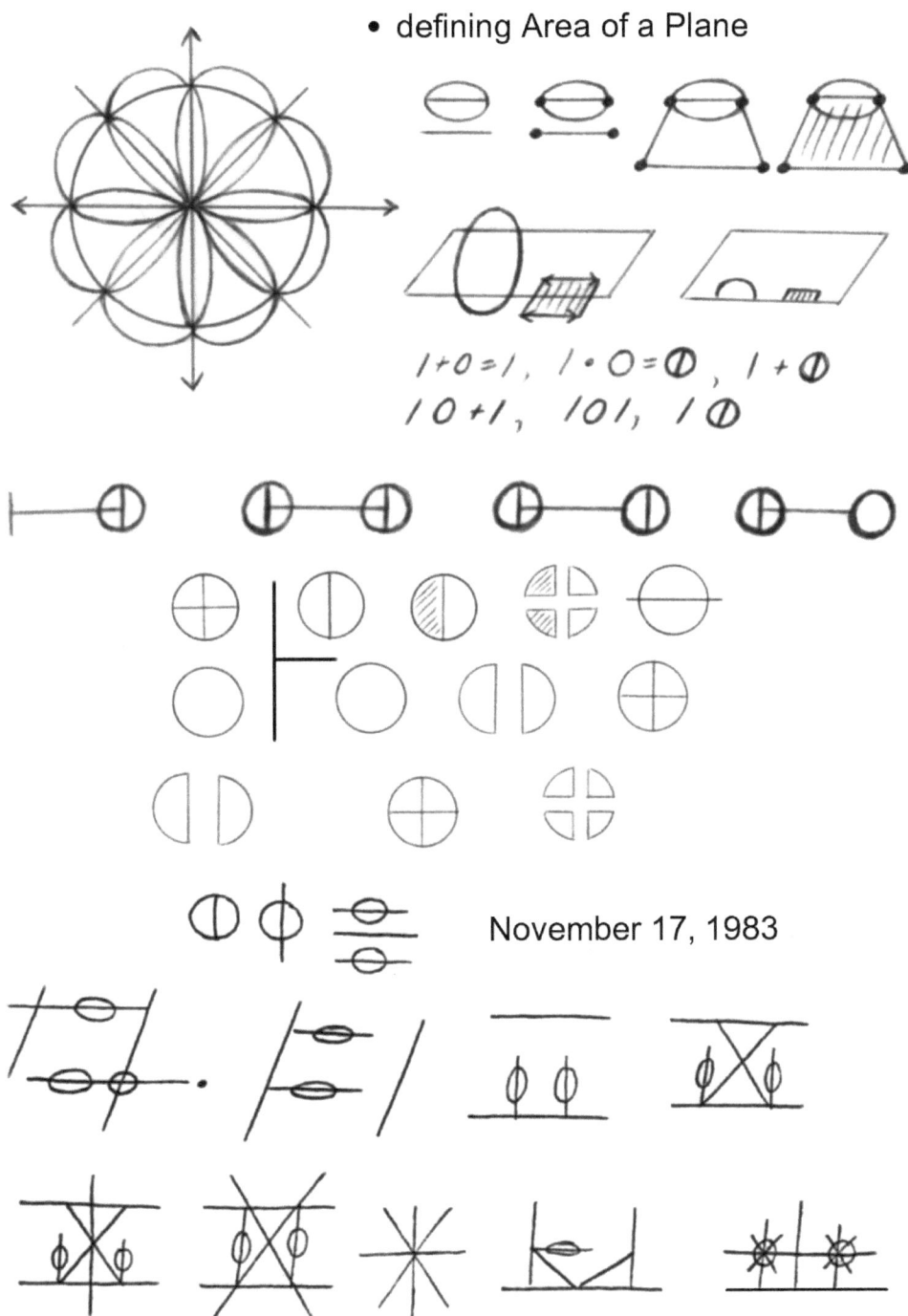

November 17, 1983

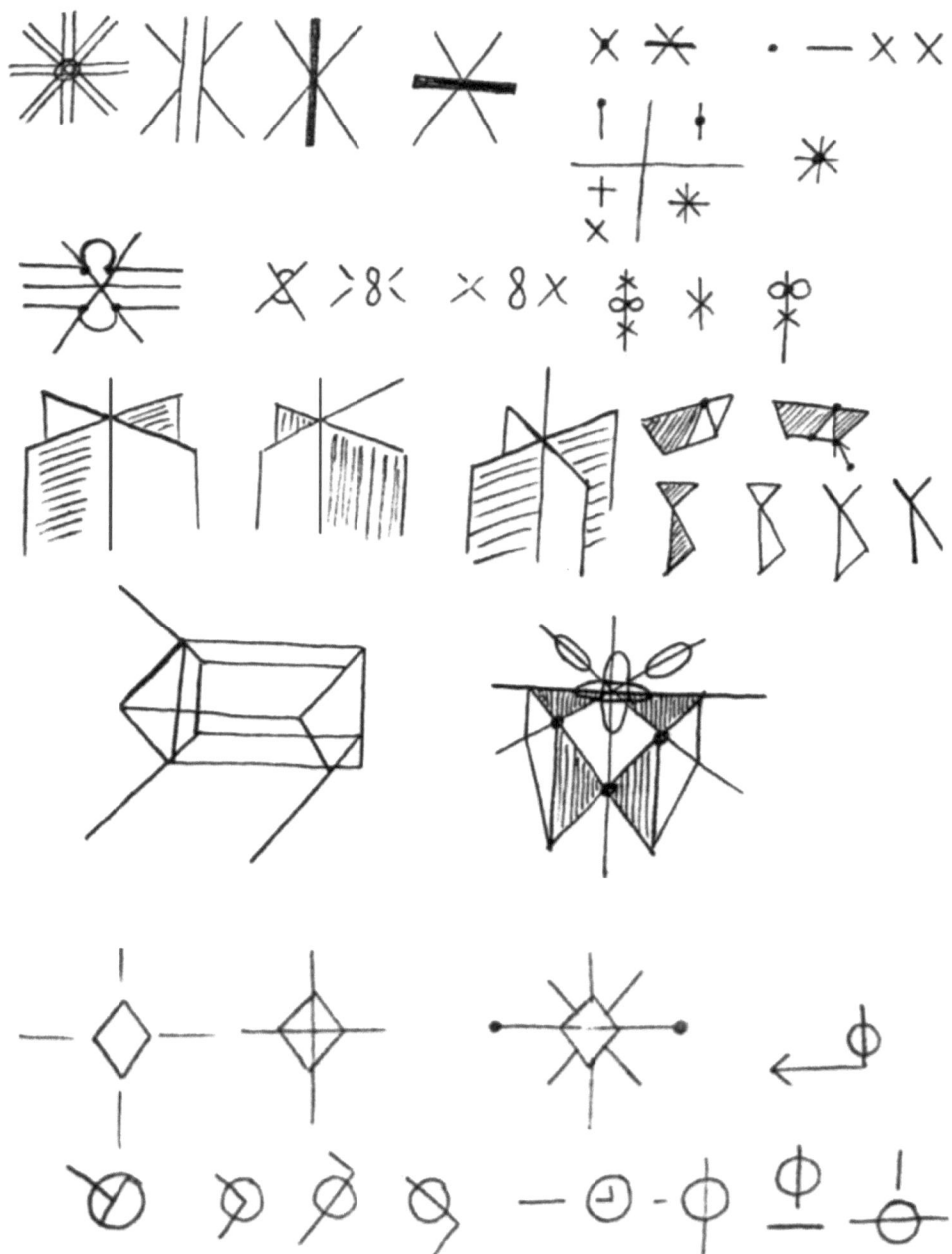

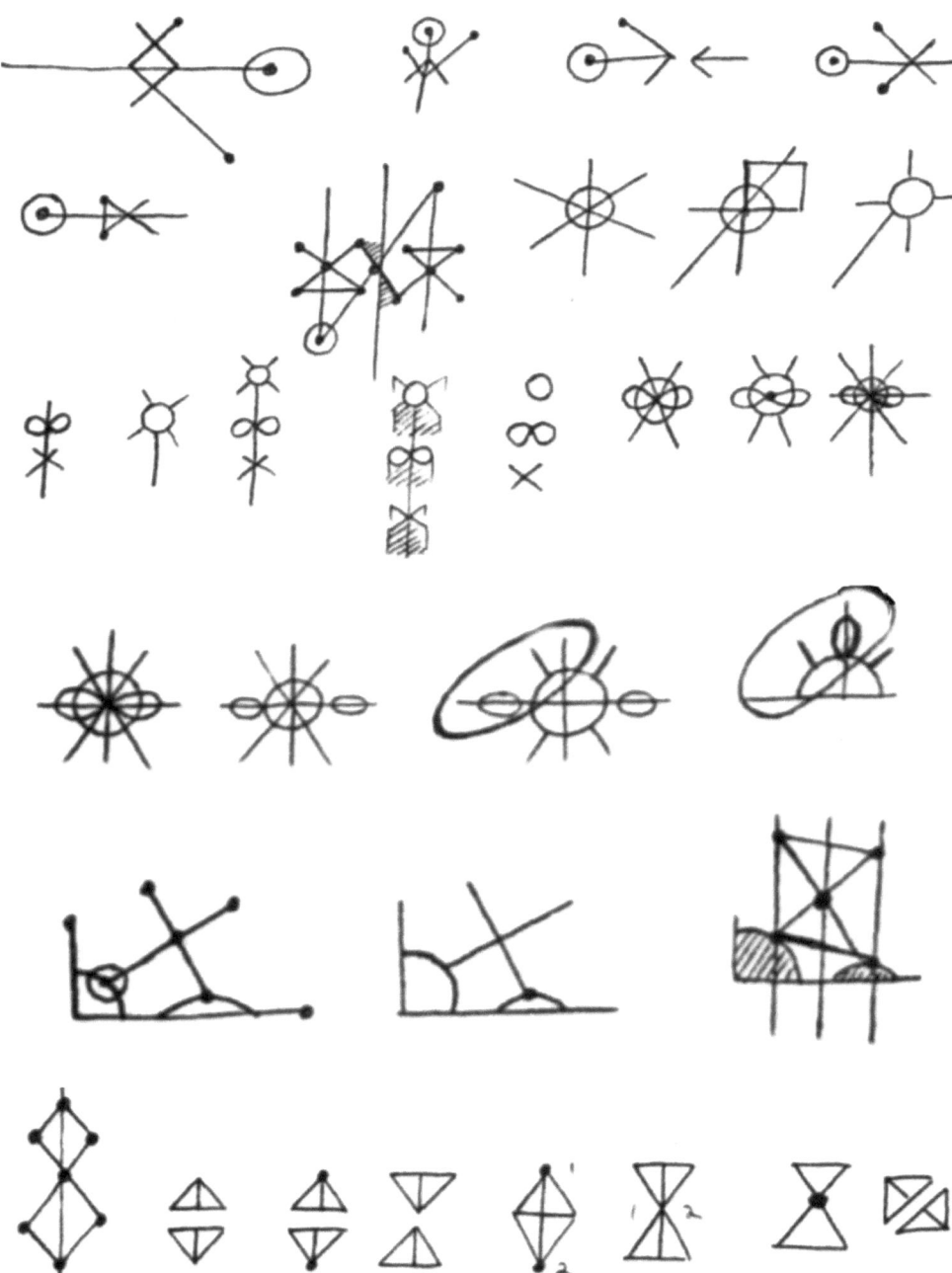

Star Script — First Viewer 5th D

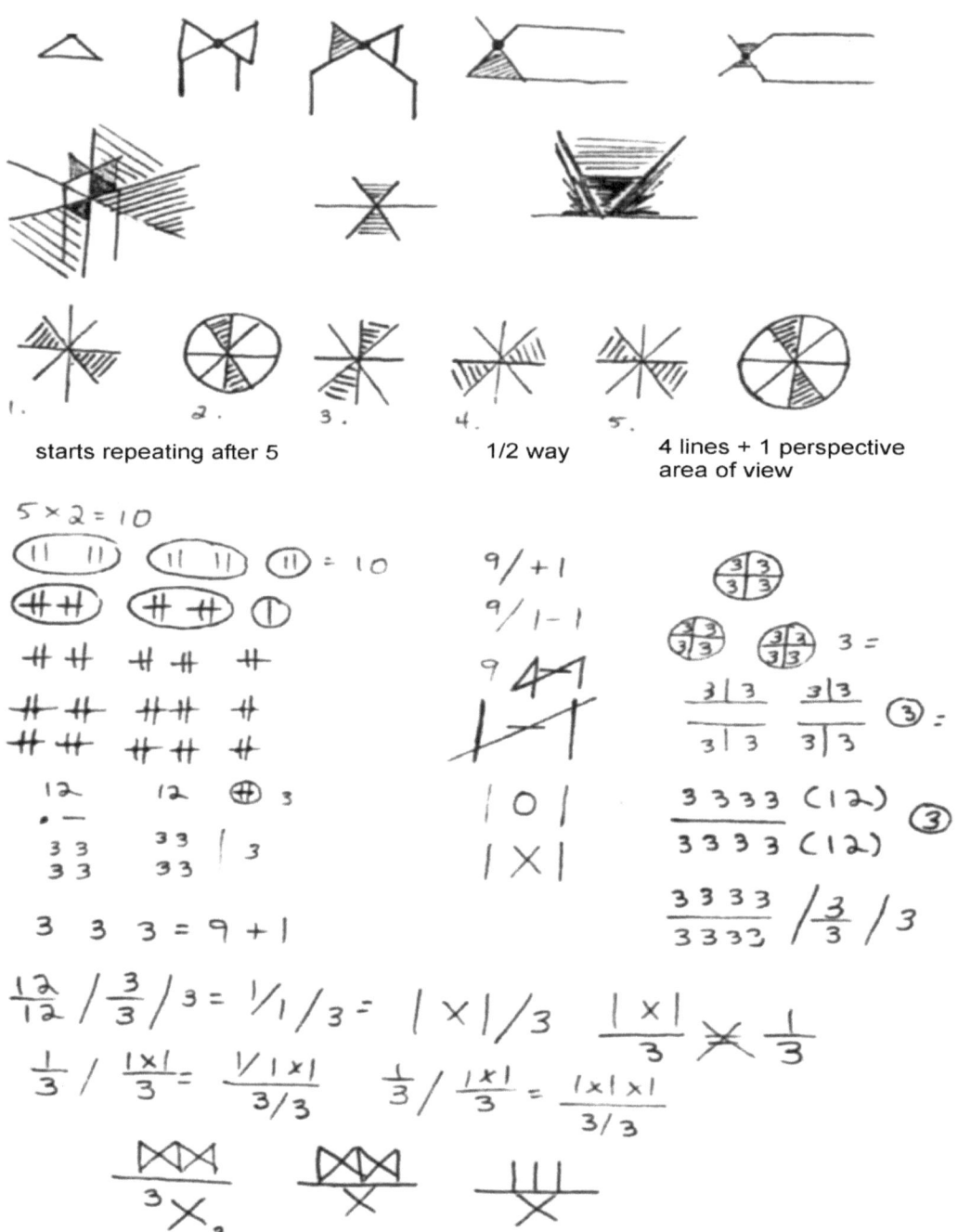

starts repeating after 5   1/2 way   4 lines + 1 perspective area of view

Star Script — First Viewer 5th D

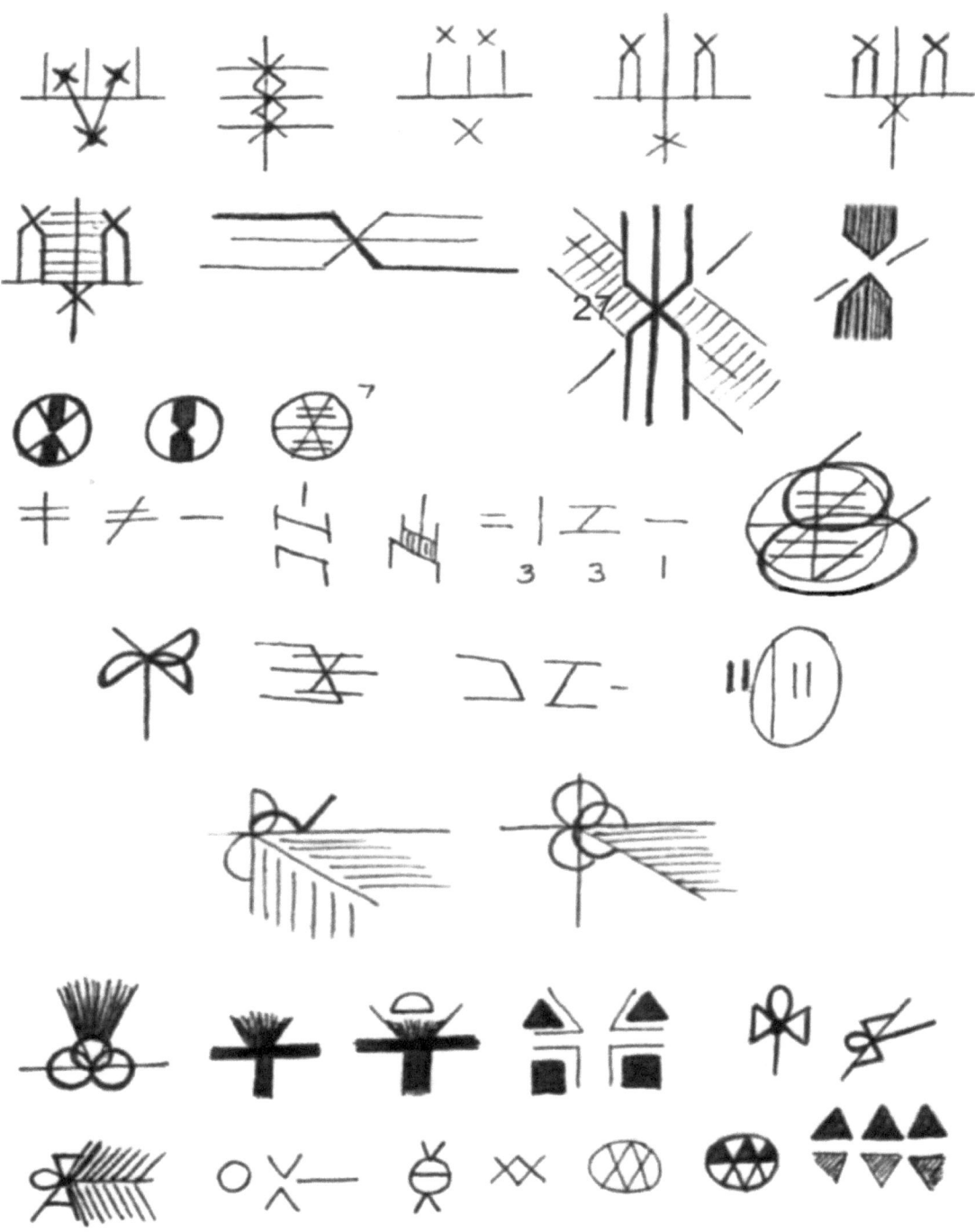

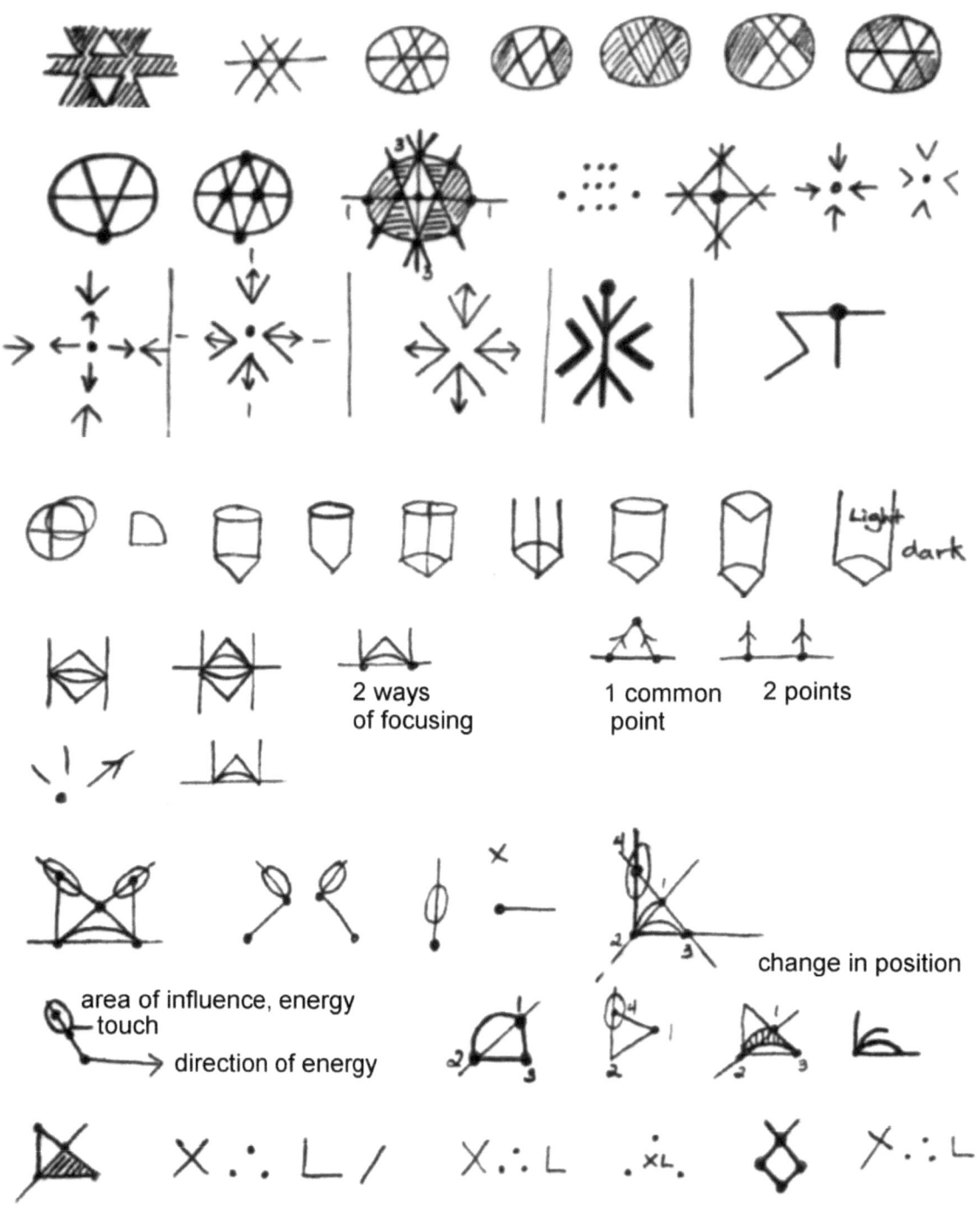

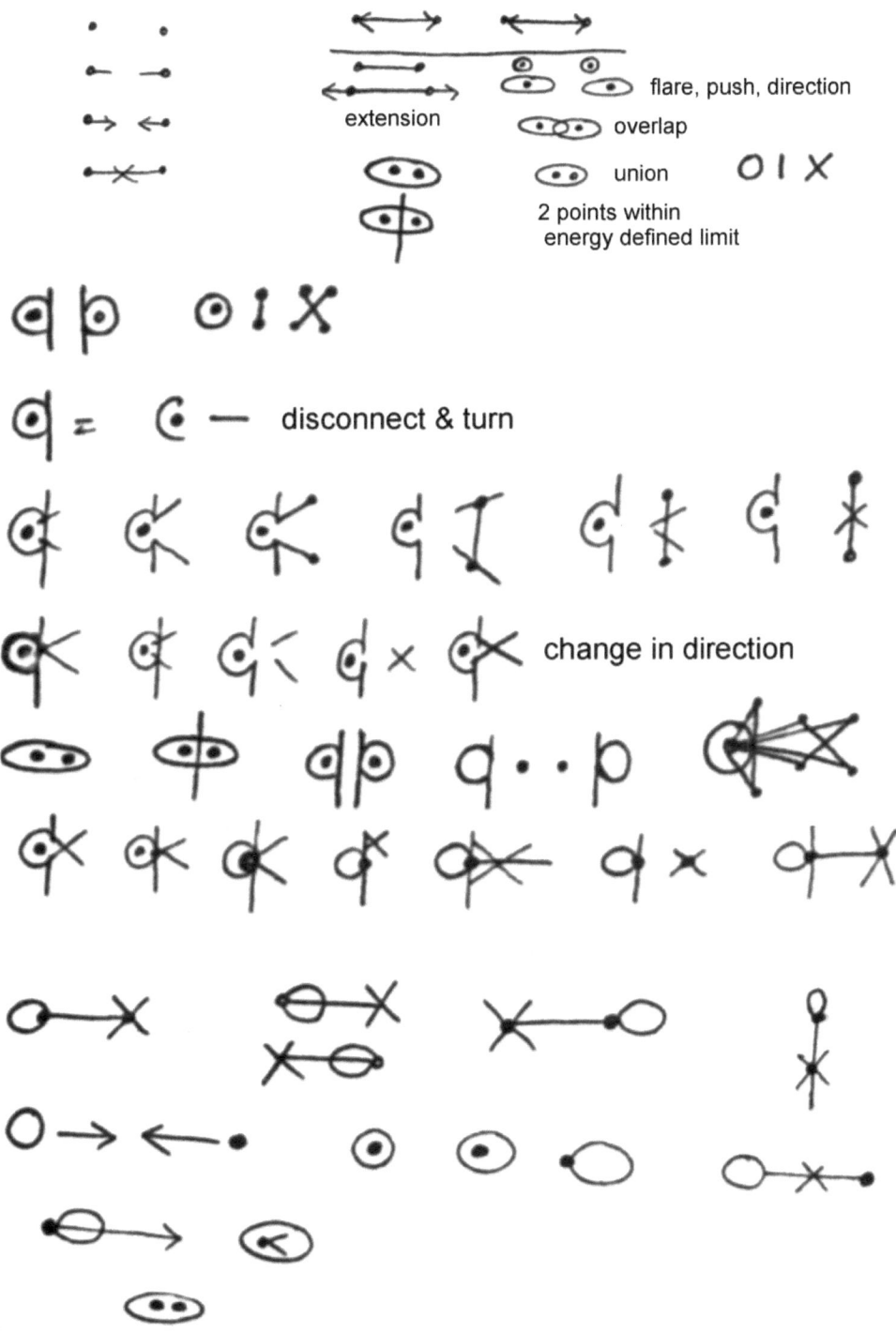

Star Script   First Viewer 5ᵗʰ D

concentration time
extended
mutual recognition
a response
direct energy focus
overlapping.
new point
being formed

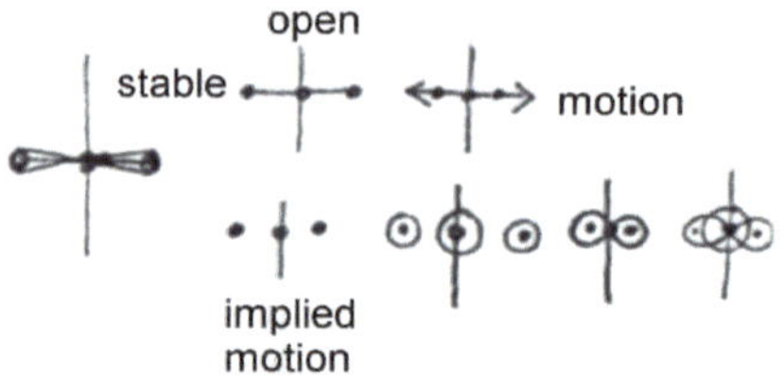

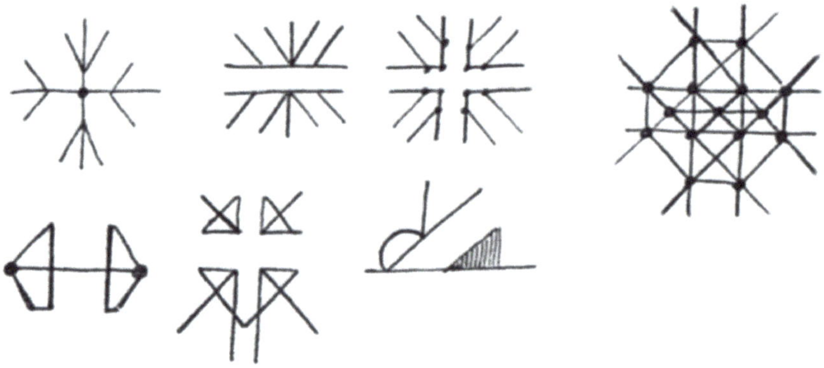

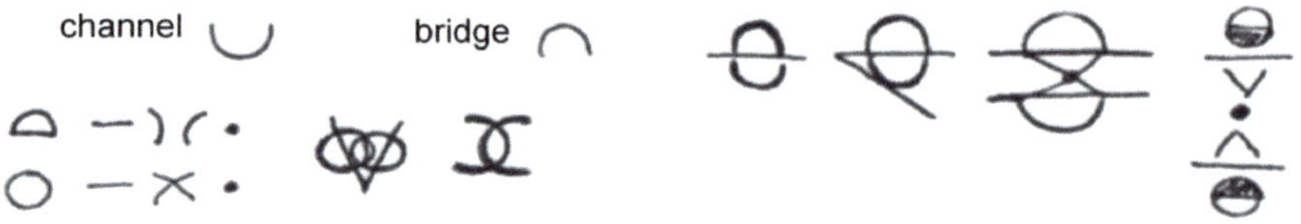

open
stable   motion
implied motion

channel ⌣   bridge ⌒

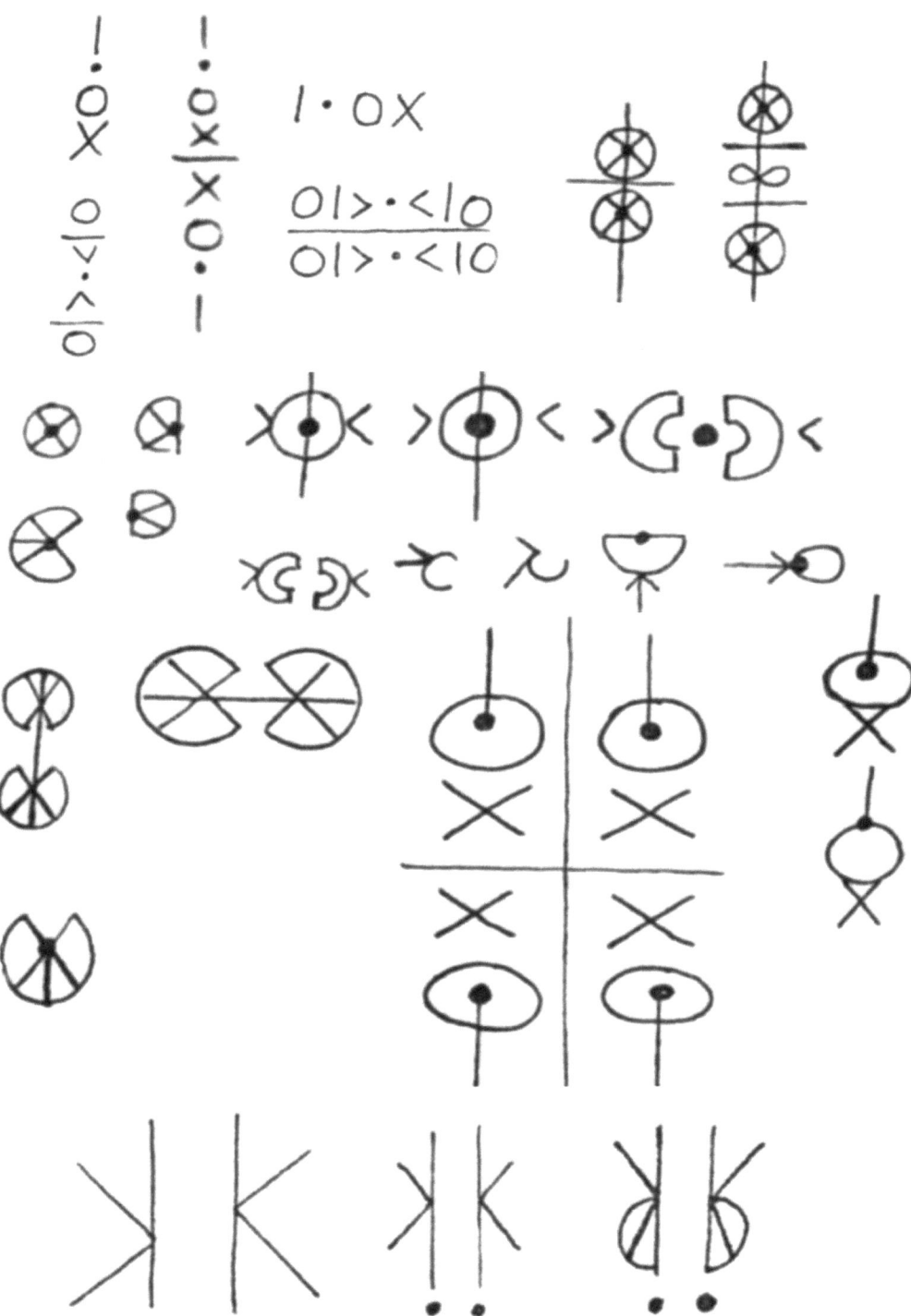

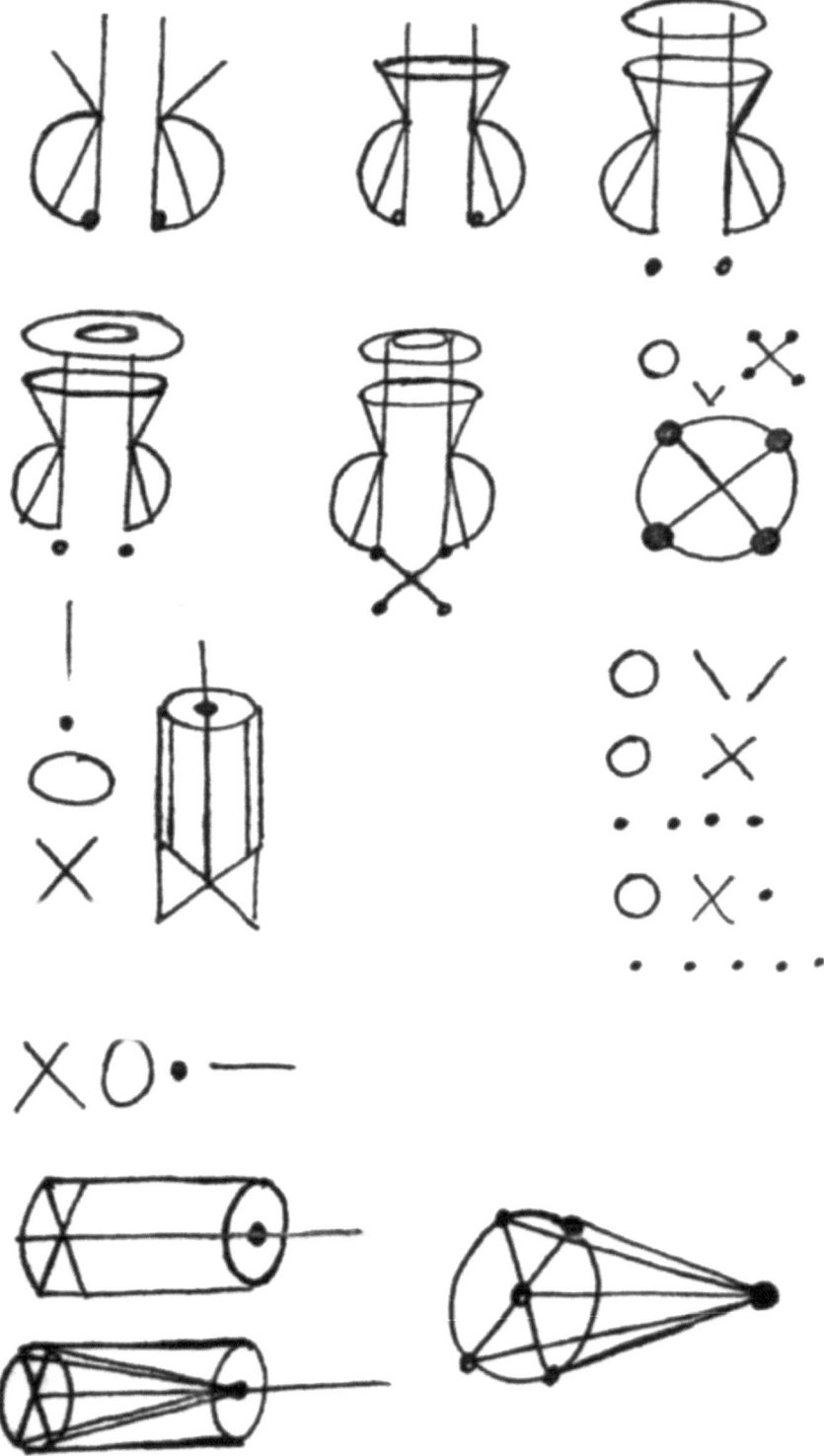

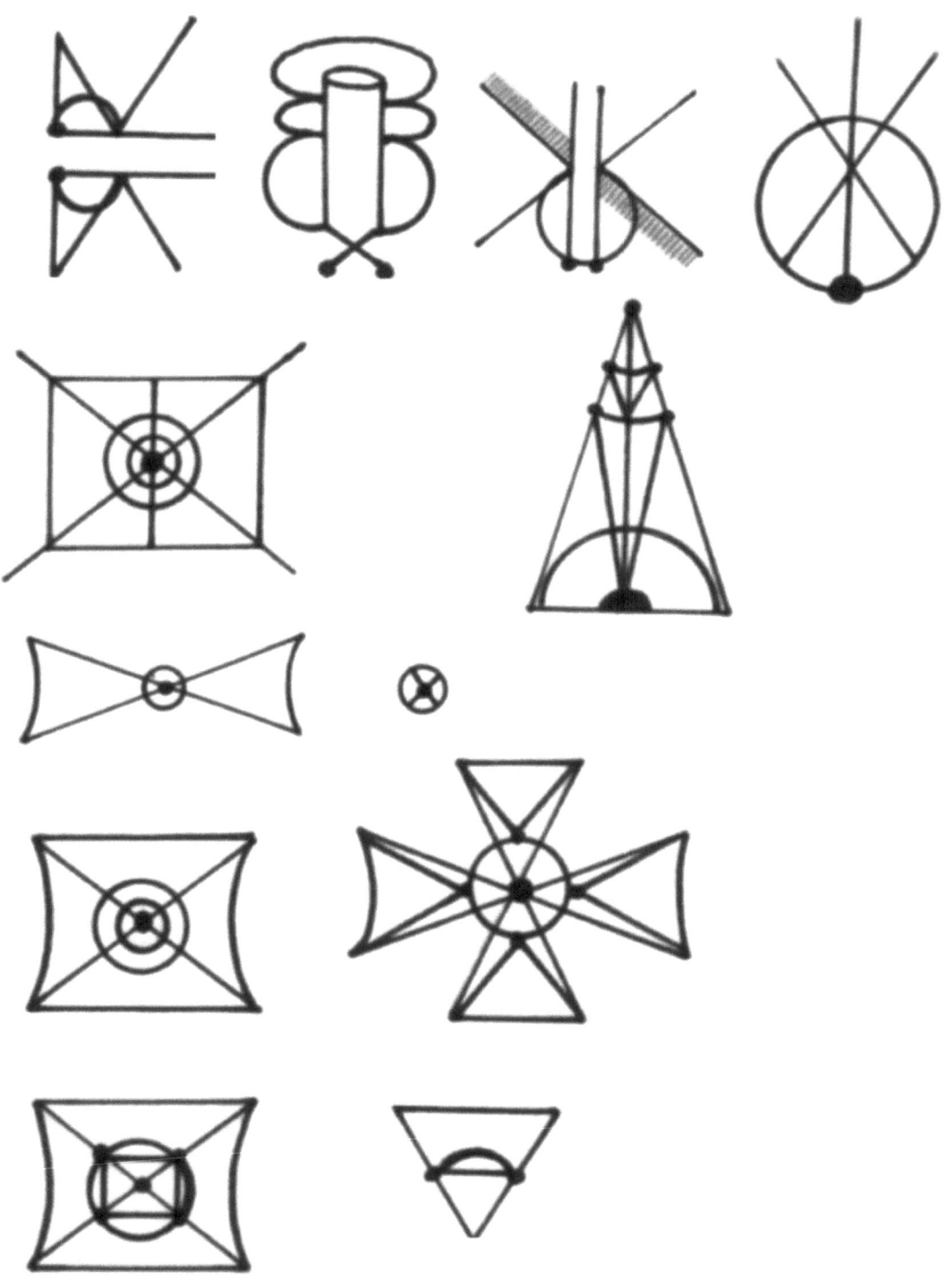

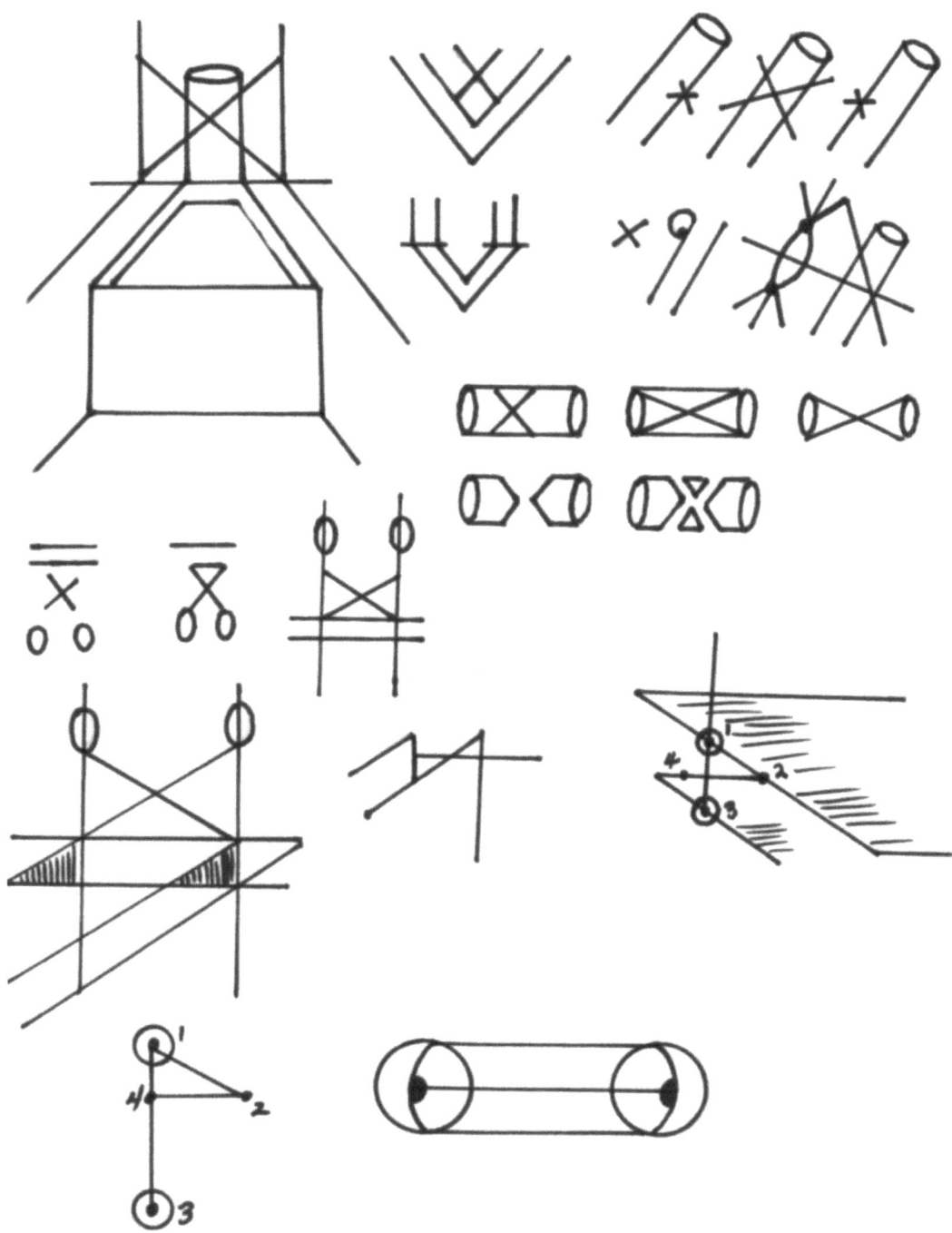

Star Script

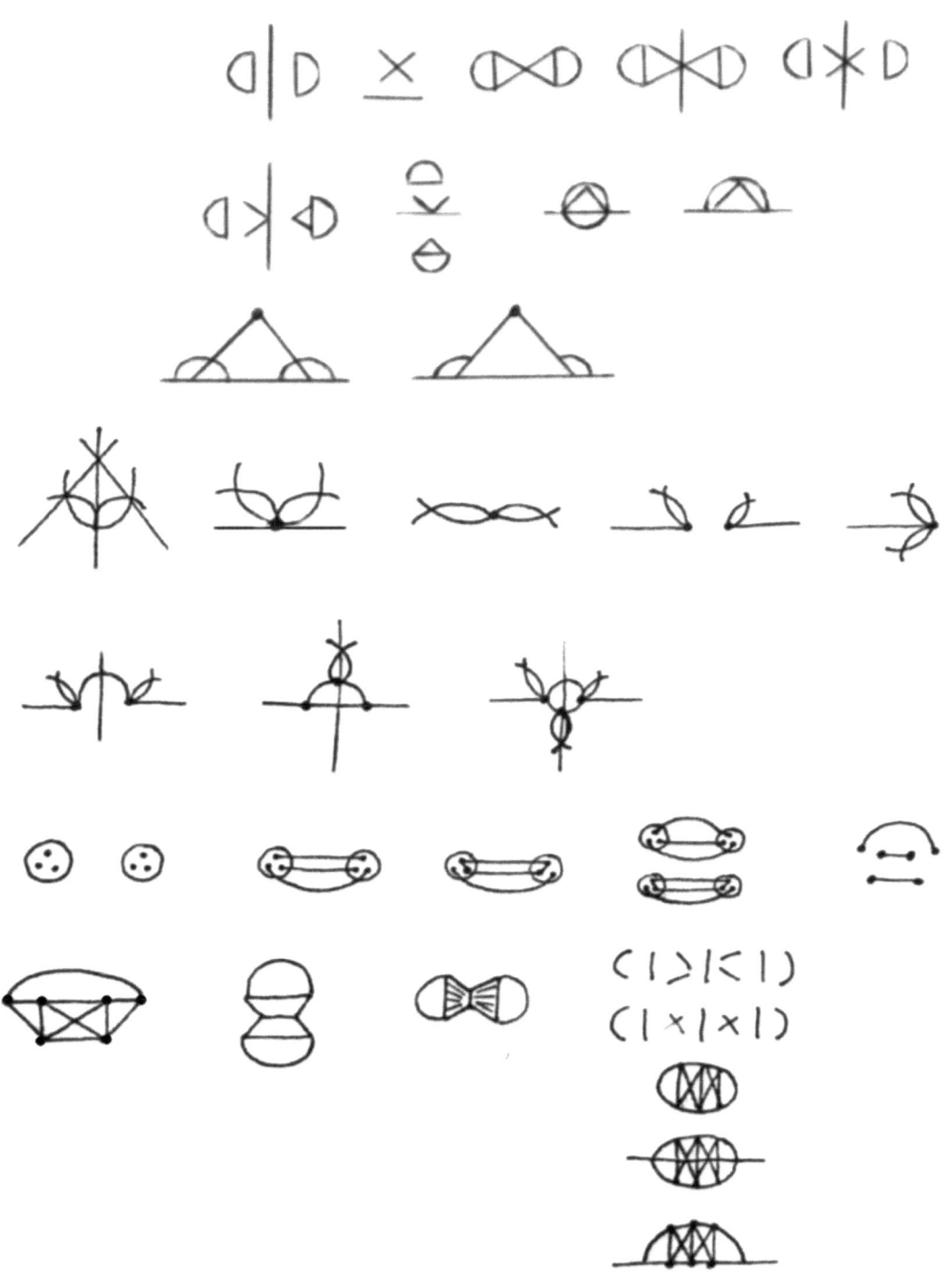

Star Script — First Viewer 5th D

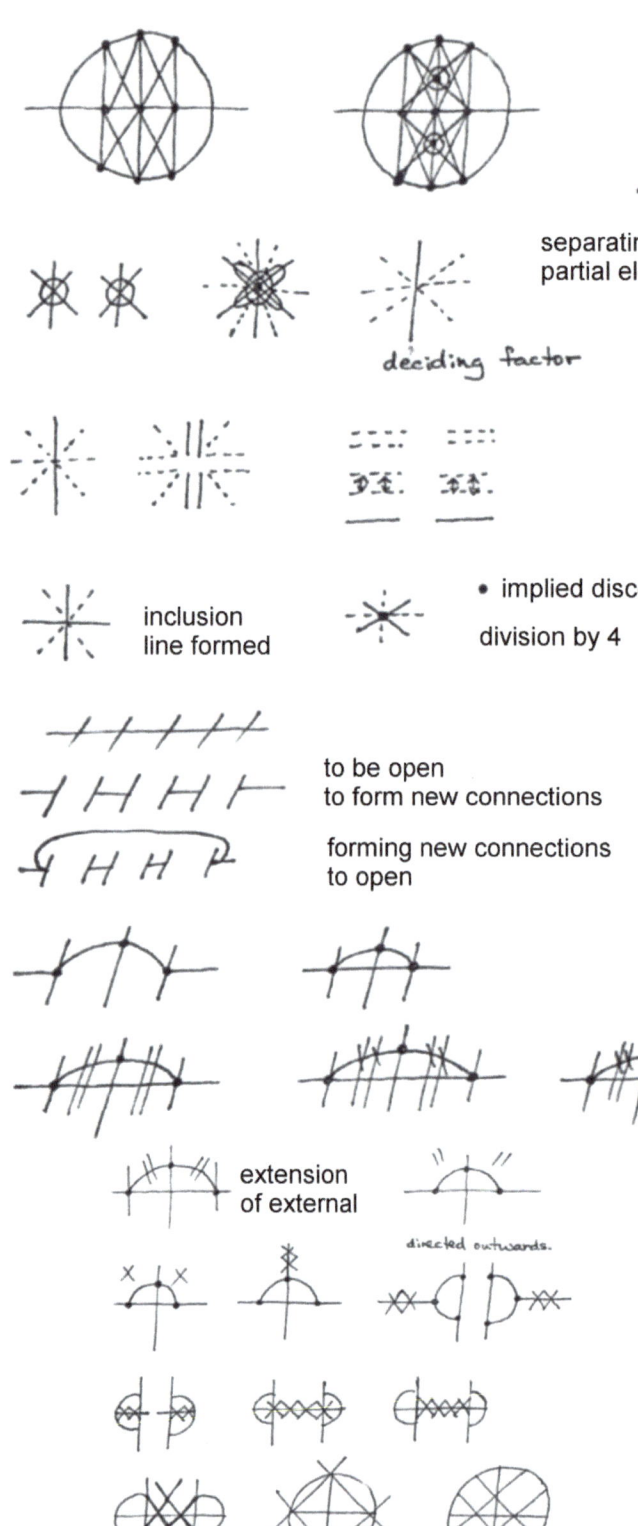

separating partial elements

deciding factor

inclusion line formed

• implied discontinuity
division by 4

to be open to form new connections

forming new connections to open

extension of external

directed outwards.

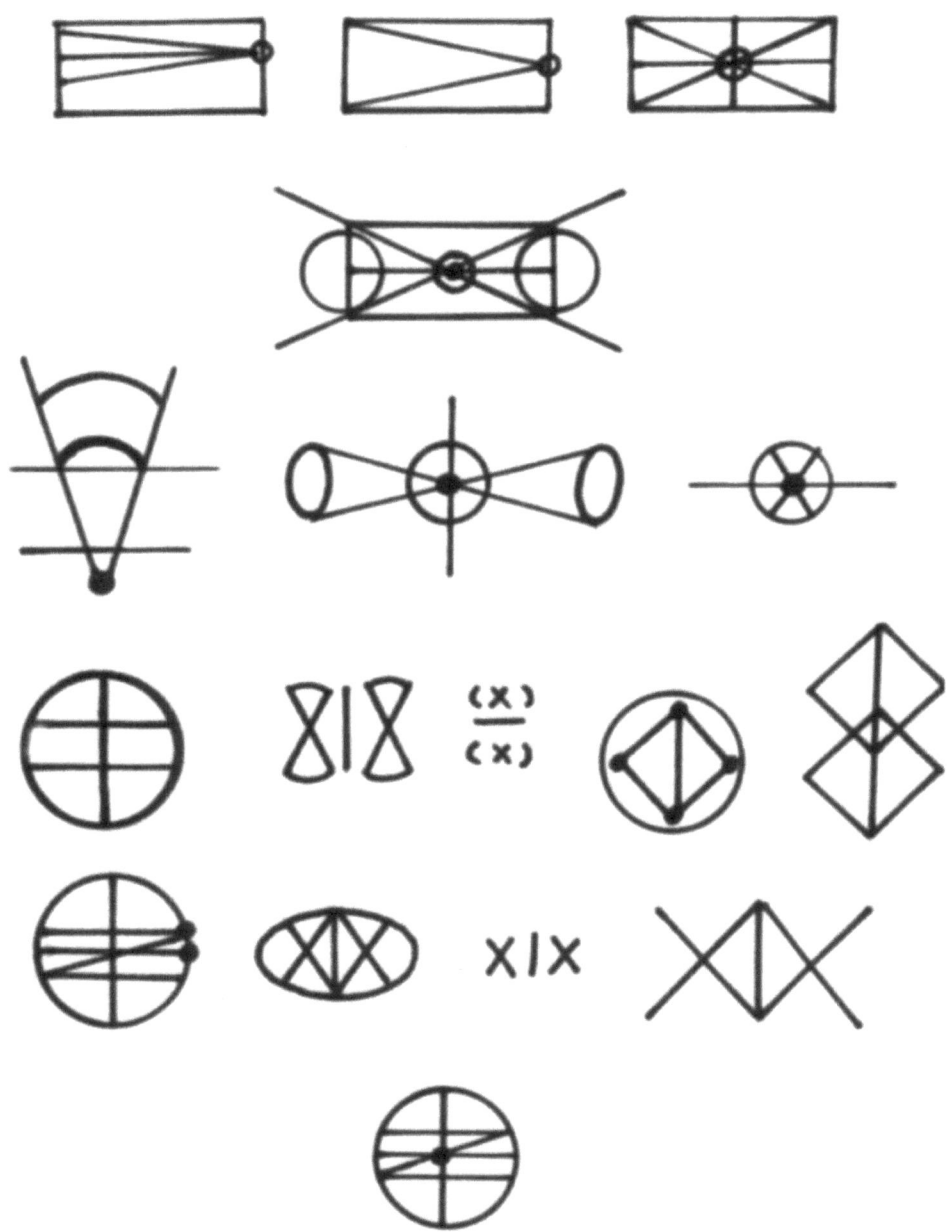

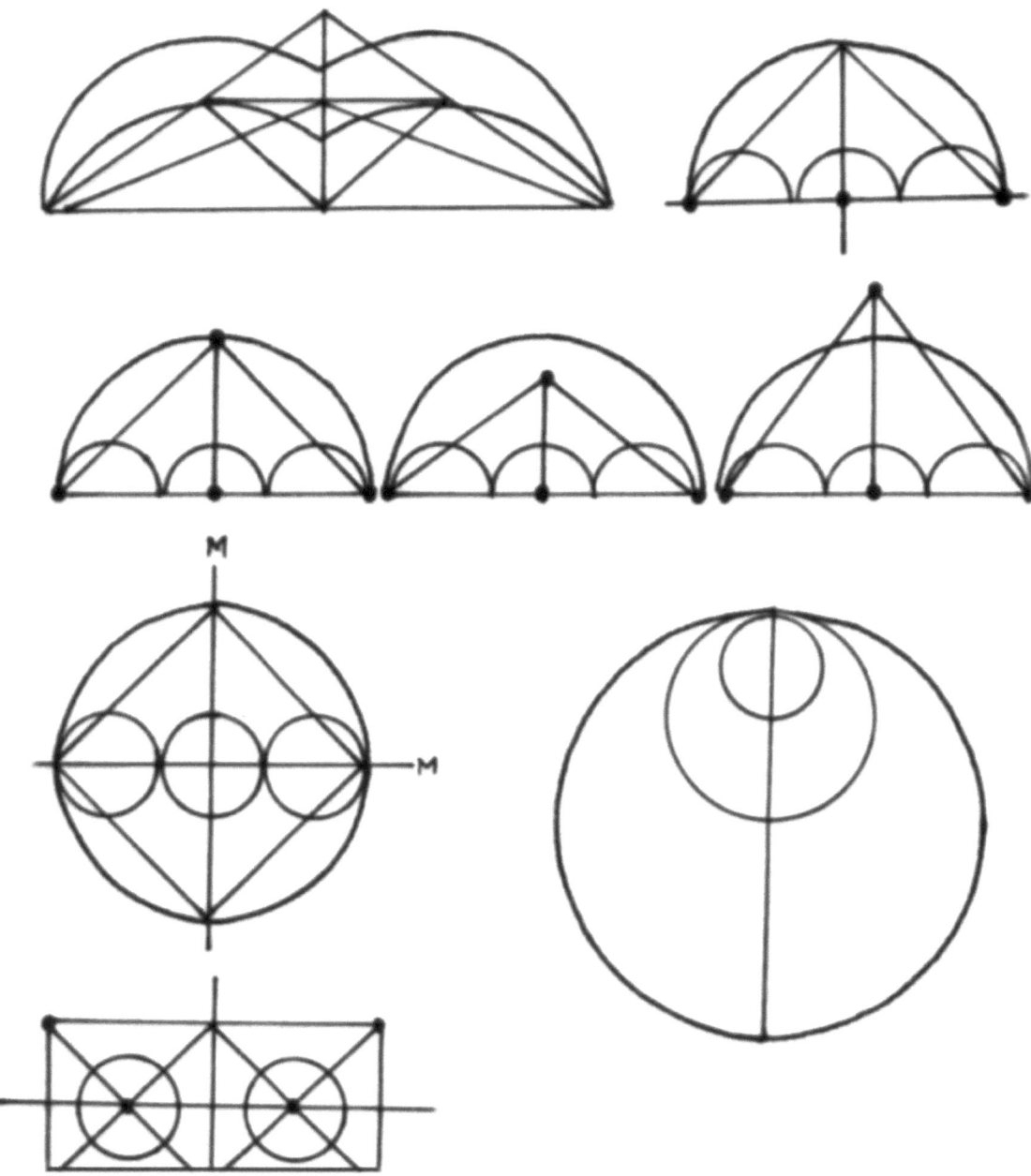

Star Script First Viewer 5th D

Sept. 4/83

a system of 4 beams of energy directed towards 1 pt.

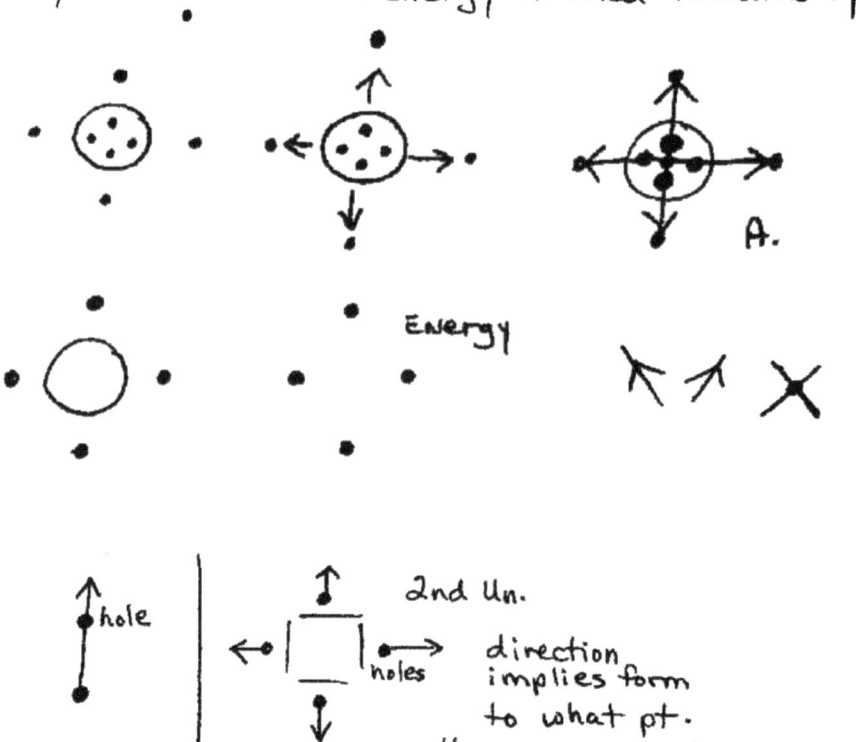

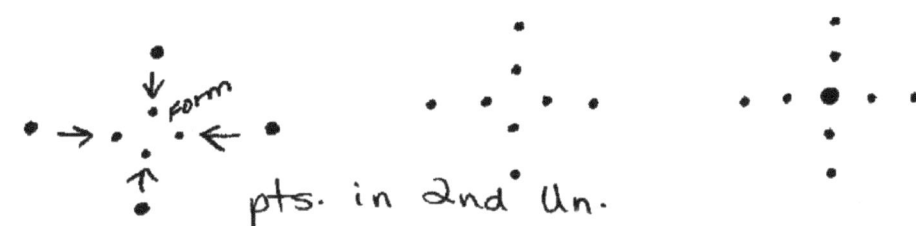

pts. in 2nd Un.

(no real change in direction of energy. internal direction is directed externally.)
- moving towards same pt. as beginning.
to the source.

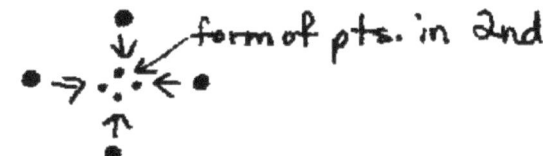
form of pts. in 2nd

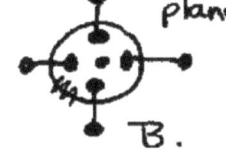
planets

B.

moving from A to B implies common source.

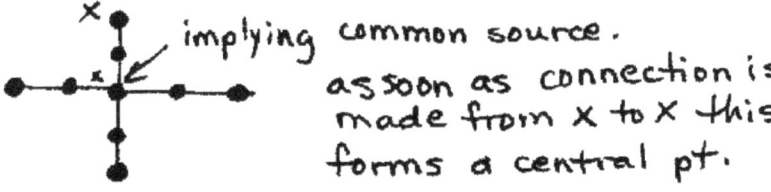
implying common source.
as soon as connection is made from x to x this forms a central pt.

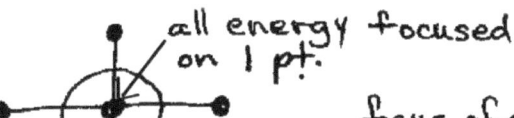
all energy focused on 1 pt.

focus of energy = star.
Blending of 4 systems into One.

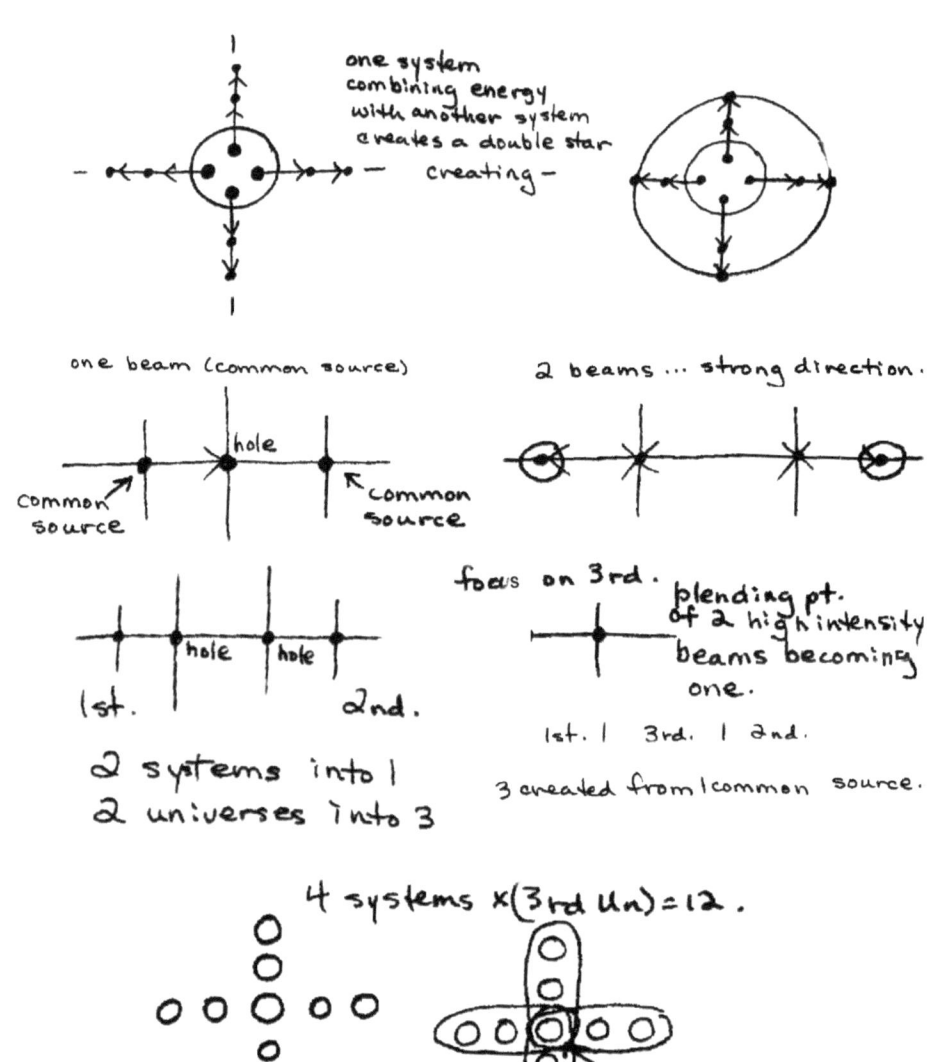

one system combining energy with another system creates a double star — creating —

one beam (common source)

2 beams ... strong direction.

hole

common source   common source

focus on 3rd.
blending pt. of 2 high intensity beams becoming one.

1st.   hole   hole   2nd.

1st. | 3rd. | 2nd.

2 systems into 1
2 universes into 3

3 created from 1 common source.

4 systems × (3rd Un) = 12.

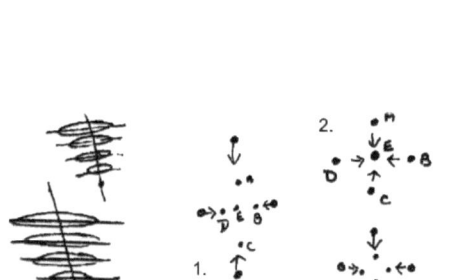

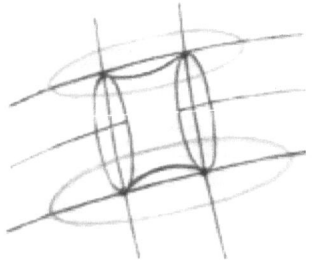

Star Script — First Viewer 5th D

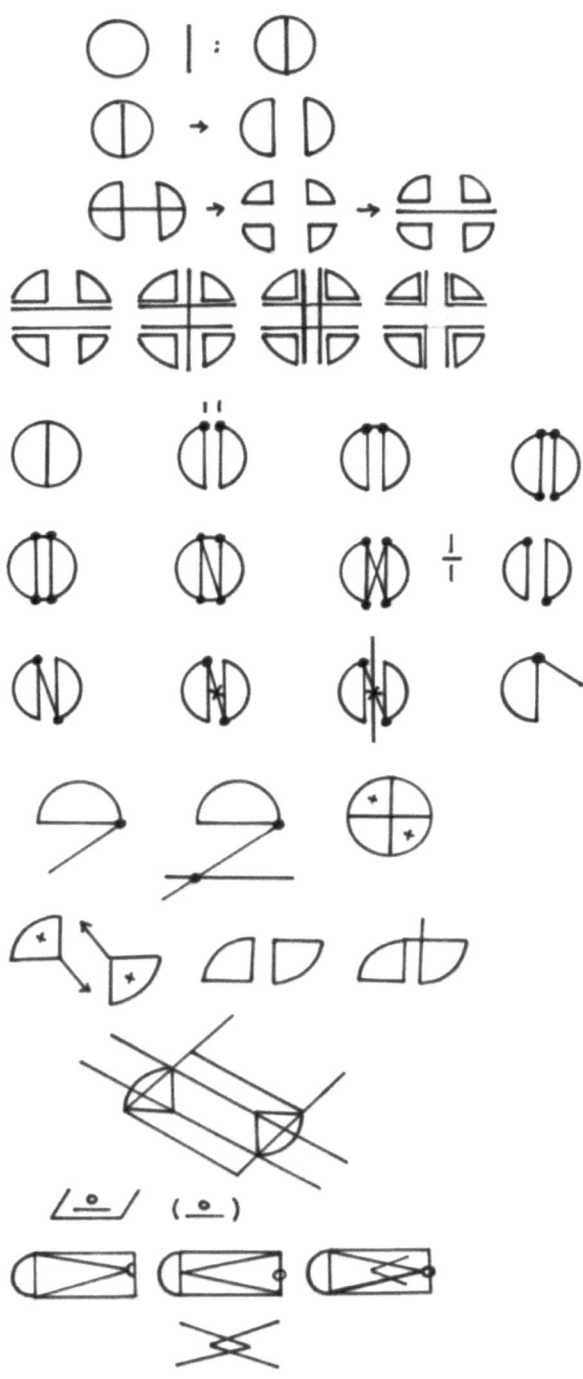

Star Script   First Viewer 5th D   78

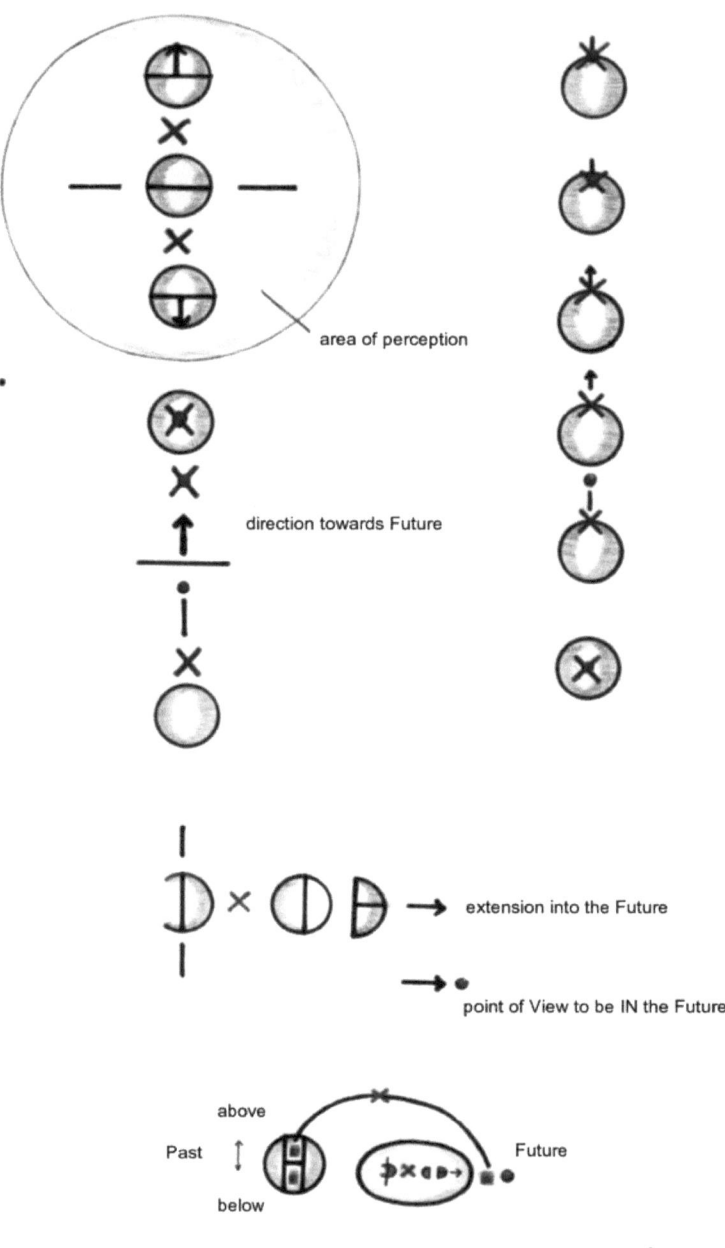

area of perception

direction towards Future

extension into the Future

point of View to be IN the Future

above
Past   Future
below

Direction 'positive'

Star Script   First Viewer 5th D   79

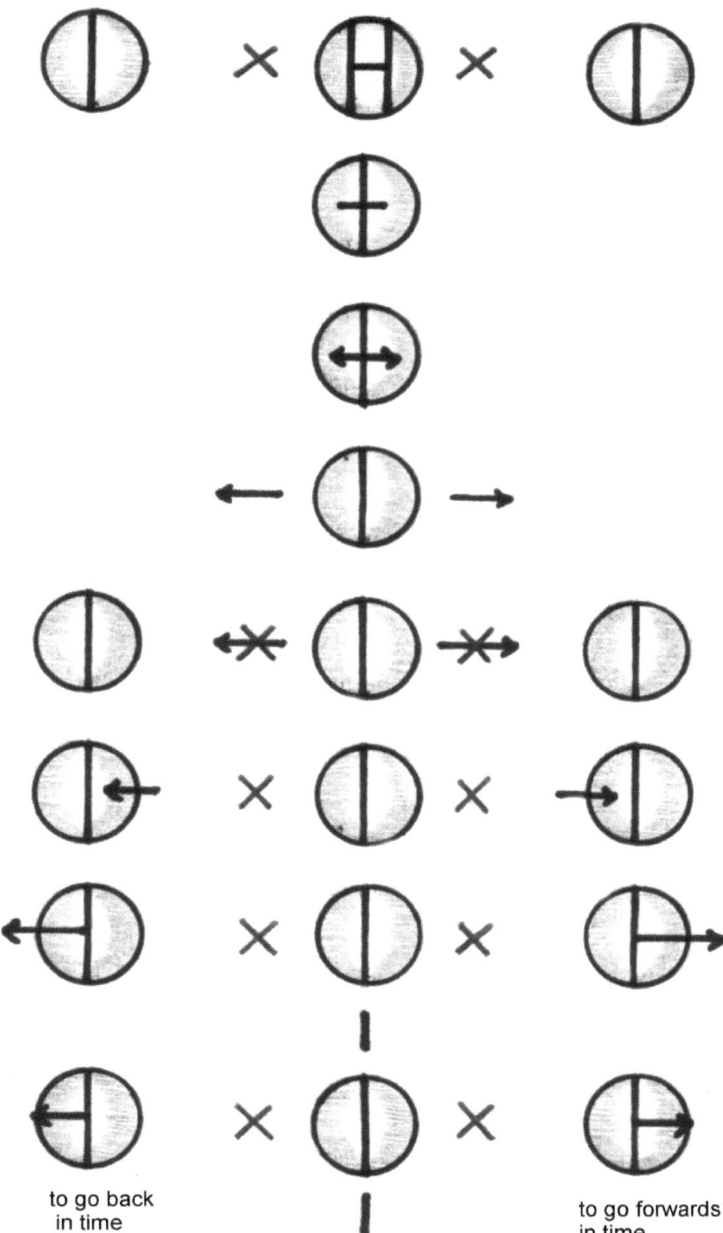

Star Script First Viewer 5th D 80

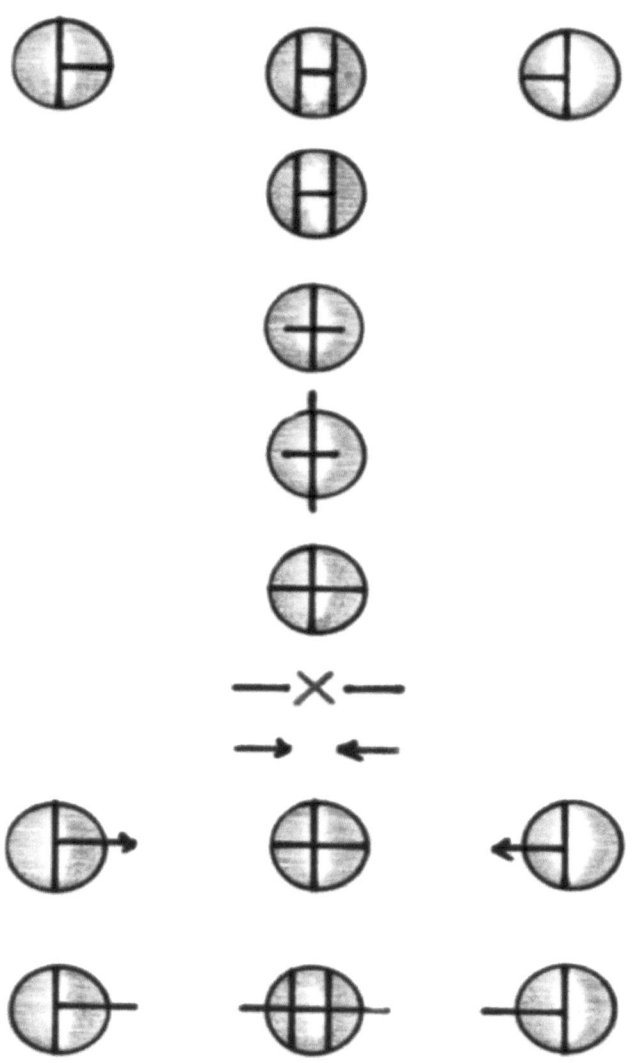

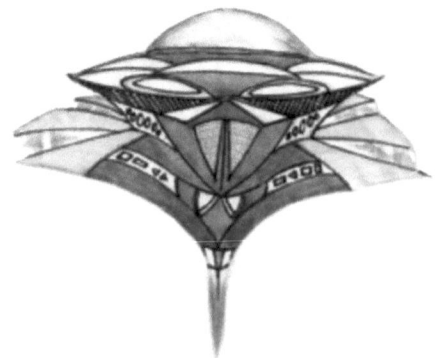

extension of time into timeless

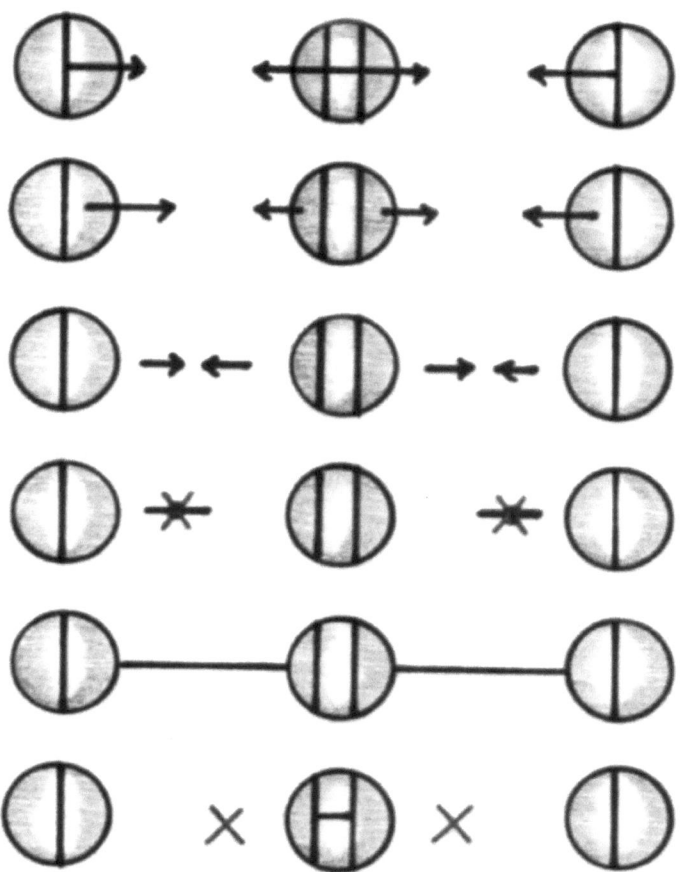

Star Script — First Viewer 5th D

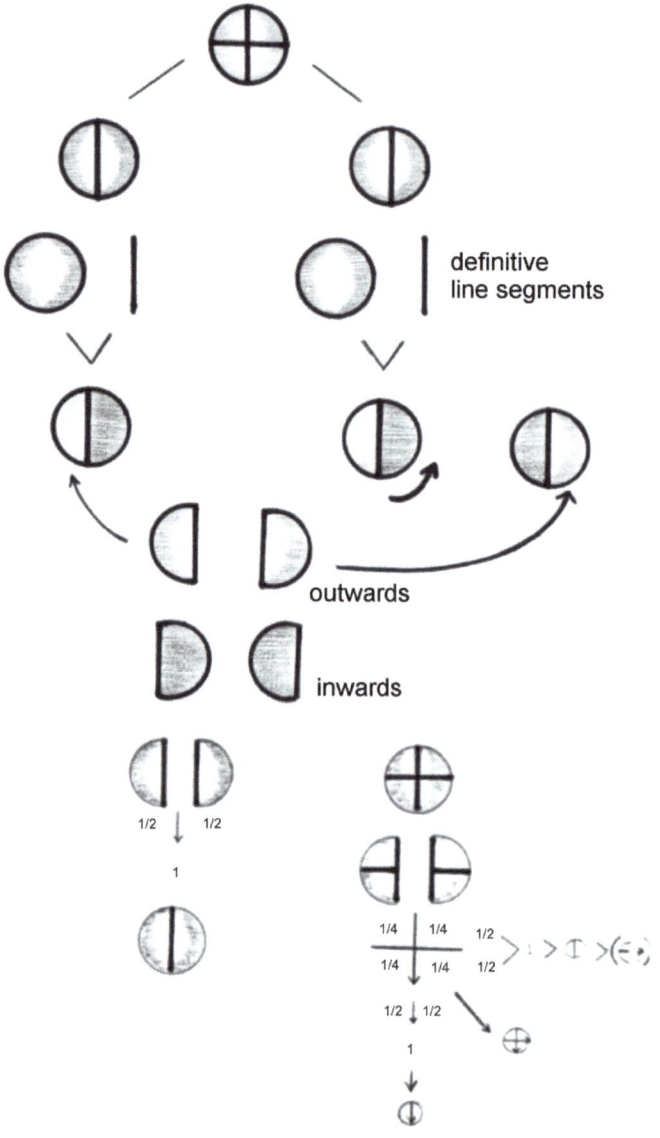

definitive line segments

outwards

inwards

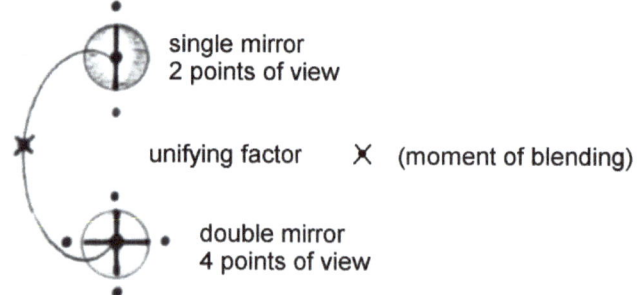

single mirror
2 points of view

unifying factor   X   (moment of blending)

double mirror
4 points of view

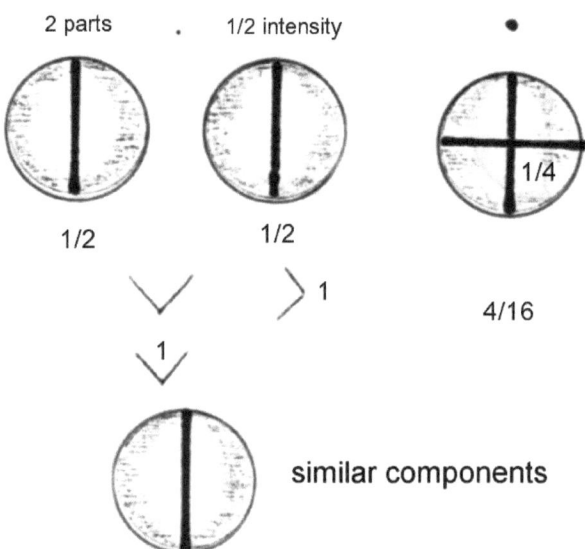

similar components

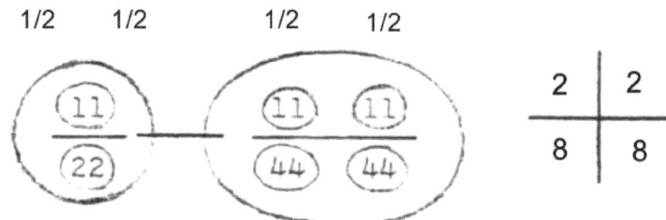

2	2
8	8

Hypercube
8+12+12 edges
24 ordinary faces
8 hyperfaces
16 vertices

$$\frac{2}{4} + \frac{2}{4} = \frac{4}{8}$$

$$\frac{2}{8} + \frac{2}{8} = \frac{4}{16}$$

$$\frac{4}{8} + \frac{4}{16} = \frac{8}{24}$$

being 16   being 8   = 1 1/2

Star Script First Viewer 5th D 84

Sept. 22nd, 1983

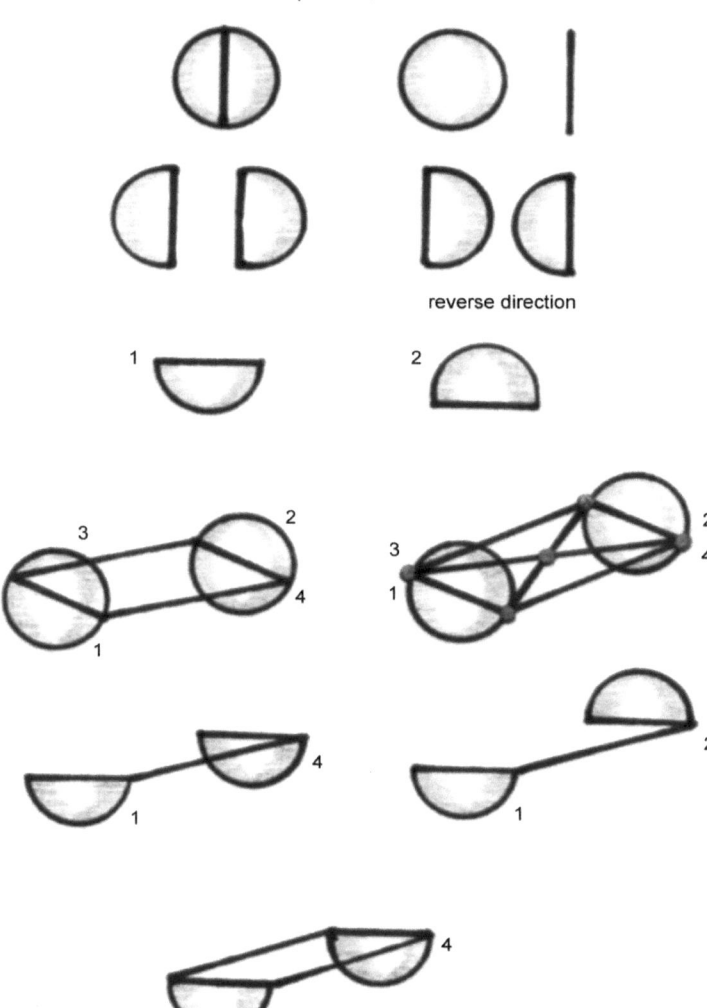

reverse direction

Our usual perception of events, substantiated and reinforced by our belief that time runs in only one direction, pre-Quantum, could be shown as:

past |————————↘|— — — — — —↘| - - - - -→ infinity
                present   future

However, understanding time as capable of running forwards and backwards like the perceptual shift inherent in hypershift, line of sight reversals, could be shown as:

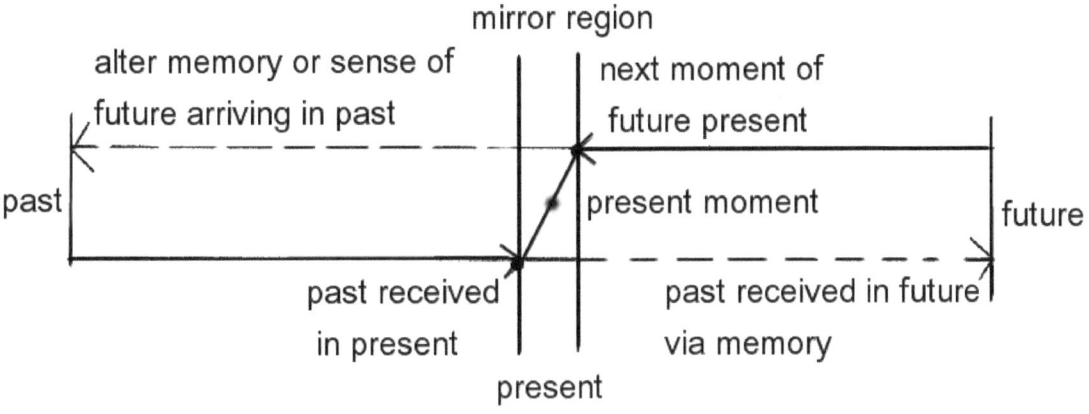

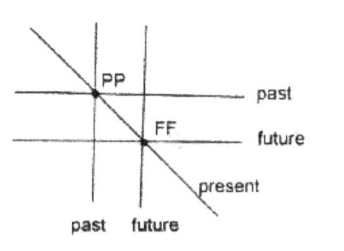 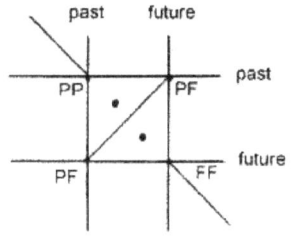 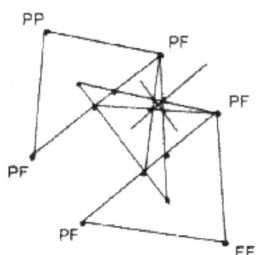

Inter-linear/dimensional (inclusive) motion between inter co-ordinated elements of an alternate reality's time, through spatial relation. (In other words, it depends on where the point of time is, in regards to the other reality as to 'what time it is').
Confluent portals

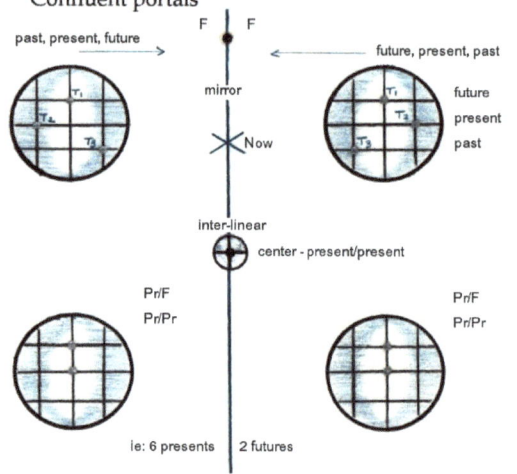

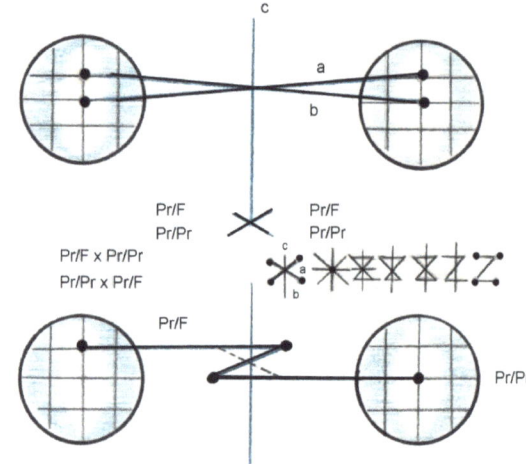

Single   Pr F x Pr/Pr 1 F, 3 Pr
        Pr/Pr x Pr/F

Combined (mirror)

    Pr/F x Pr/Pr
    Pr/Pr x Pr/F   Pr/F____Pr/R
    = 2 F
     2 Pr

_____ Mirror

    Pr/F x Pr/Pr
    Pr/Pr x Pr/F   Pr/Pr____Pr/Pr
    = 4 Pr

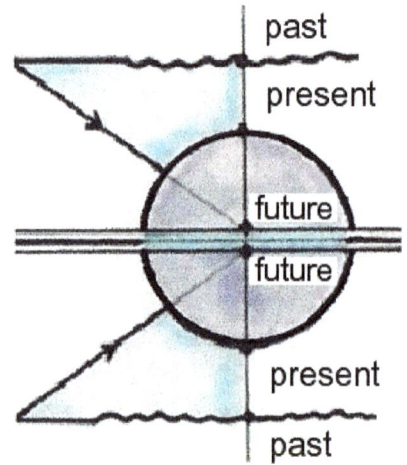